THE GENTLE ART OF
SMOKING

THE GENTLE ART OF
SMOKING

BY

ALFRED H. DUNHILL

with drawings by

JAMES ARNOLD

MAX REINHARDT

LONDON

First published September 1954
Reprinted November 1954

Set in Bembo and printed by
THE STELLAR PRESS
BARNET HERTS

CONTENTS

PLATES

DRAWINGS IN THE TEXT

INTRODUCTION

It is not necessary to be a member of the Tobacco Trade to realise that the world-wide practice of smoking is rapidly becoming, except for a small minority, a lost art and a limited pleasure. Indeed, many smokers in the furious tempo of modern life have freely admitted that it is only an essential narcotic for frayed nerves. For them choice Havana cigars, hand-made cigarettes and lustrous meerschaum pipes, which graced the smoking-rooms of fifty years ago, must seem almost as remote as the elaborate smoking paraphernalia which brought such excitement to Elizabethan England. To-day the ubiquitous cigarette has robbed most of us of these former glories and gripped us by the throat. Smoking has become habit, and habit, proverbially, blunts the edge of pleasure.

To one whose business it is to interest the public in the whole realm of smoking, all this is a very great pity. Yet it is not wholly explained by the economic problems of the day. He who smokes at all can afford to vary the way in which he smokes and to learn a little more about the pleasure which, to say the least of it, is expensive enough. But having tried to cater for the whims and caprices of smokers for many years, I am sure that a little sound knowledge of tobacco and some spirit of adventure are the very qualities that the majority of smokers lack. Deeply conservative, so many are prepared to pay large annual sums without considering how they may get the most enjoyment in return. Smoking is held to be something that you learn about instinctively, or a habit that requires little investigation. People with such an attitude shut their eyes to what they spend and what they smoke. As a result, cigars are bought, mishandled and sometimes wasted. Pipes which are the product of many years of skill and craftsmanship are bought by people who have little more than fancy to guide their choice, and smoked in ways that make it impossible for them to give satisfaction. Some brands of tobacco give delight to a few, but are never sampled by the majority. Cigarettes are sometimes selected as though the only distinguishing feature was the colour and shape of the box.

Nor is all this surprising, for the prolific literature on the subject of smoking (a great deal of which is now out of date) has seldom passed beyond the libraries of experts and has concerned itself very little with the practical problems that interest smokers. Age is set in its ways, and the very young, it seems to me, have increasing difficulty in finding a guide in what was once considered to be an art. I have therefore attempted to write a book which, in a short compass, could never be comprehensive, but which sets out to be historical, technical and practical. It is, I like to think, an adequate introduction to the whole subject and those who detect its limitations will find more comprehensive works on particular branches of the subject in the bibliography. Perhaps the most valuable part of the book is the chapter headed ' The Practice of Smoking ' because there I have attempted to collate the experience of men who have spent years in dealing with the practical problems of individual smokers. It may help those who are not connoisseurs to buy, to enjoy and look after their tobacco, pipes and cigars.

I should add that I am not an historian. The whole subject of smoking, which has interested me for many years, has been pursued by scholars more ardent and learned than I. It has been sufficient for my present purpose to give some account of their findings and, when in doubt about historical matters, to accept the judgment of the majority. The History of Pipes, for example, is based largely on the evidence of the Dunhill Collection which was collated by my father in ' The Pipe Book '– a work which is now unfortunately out of print. To anyone who has read widely in the history of smoking I must admit at the outset that I have little new to offer.

Grateful acknowledgements are made to many friends who have given me valuable advice and information. I must mention in particular Mr Alexander Black, who provided most helpful notes on the chapters concerned with tobacco, and Mr L. Waddington who, as an expert on the manufacture of snuff, read the chapter on that subject and made many valuable suggestions. Thanks are due to Mr C. McConnell who helped me to obtain some of the technical photographs, and to the owners of other photographs who have allowed them to be reproduced among the illustrations.

CHAPTER I

THE HISTORY OF SMOKING

'... I know, I feel, that with the introduction of tobacco England woke up from a long sleep... The glory of existence became a thing to speak of. Men who had hitherto only concerned themselves with the narrow things of home put a pipe into their mouths and became philosphers.'

SIR JAMES BARRIE *My Lady Nicotine*

¶ *The Origin*

Some modern scholars have argued that the word ' Tobacco ' is derived from the Arabic word ' Tubbaq ' and that the practice of smoking tobacco which, they say, was known in the Near and Far East in ancient times, spread to West Africans through whom it found its way into America possibly a century before the so-called discovery. If this were so, it is odd that such early explorers as Vasco da Gama and Marco Polo should make no reference to the smoking of tobacco in the Orient before 1500, while later explorers, who followed the Dutch, English and Portuguese traders into Asia in the seventeeth century, make frequent reference to it. In fact other historians have shown more convincingly that it was these seventeenth century traders who spread the habit of smoking tobacco, and that the explorers were in error in thinking that tobacco was indigenous to the countries they visited. Tobacco and the tobacco pipe came, therefore, from America, and the clay pipes, sometimes unearthed in England and ascribed to the

Maya Priest Smoking: from a carving in a Maya Temple
at Palenque

ancients, are identified erroneously. At the earliest they were buried when Shakespeare was alive.

But the smoking, chewing and snuffing of plants other than tobacco was known in Europe, Asia and Africa from ancient times. In Egypt, Greece and Rome, incense purified smoke from altars and was offered to the gods. Pliny refers to the Roman use of pipes for medicinal purposes and, during the Graeco-Roman period, coltsfoot was used as a cure for asthma and also for ritualistic purposes. The Scythians of South East Europe smoked hempseed, and Pythian priests used some form of smoking for making prophesies. Yet the Saxons, Danes and Northern Germanic tribes that invaded England seem to have been ignorant of the practice.

It has been proved beyond reasonable doubt that the smoking of tobacco arose, in some remote time, from the religious ceremonies of priests in coastal districts of the countries we now know as Central America and Mexico. Stone carvings depict priests of the Mayas, a highly cultured people whose civilisation began before the birth of Christ, using a form of pipe to blow tobacco smoke towards the sun and the four points of the compass. Such practices gradually spread to other tribes in what we now call Mexico, particularly to the fabulous Aztecs who used reeds for smoking; and further north, in the ' mounds ' of the Mississippi basin, archeologists have discovered pipes of bone, wood and clay that may have been smoked for over 1,000 years before any European set foot in the country.

It is believed that the plants Nicotiana Tabacum and Nicotiana Rustica – the two species from which modern tobacco is derived – originated in Brazil and Mexico respectively, but that, long before the discovery of America, Nicotiana Rustica was growing east and west of the Mississippi and that other plants were also in North America and Eastern Canada. Since all these were rare and the Indians regarded them as gifts from the gods, their value was immense – greater than that which gold was to have on the Spanish Main. Indeed, the natives of North America and Canada were found to economise by blending their tobacco with sumac, the bark of dogswood, herbs, and oil which bound the dust together.

It is not difficult to see why the natives valued so highly the plant that was apparently capable of inducing a trance and stupefaction. Doubtless the priests persuaded their tribes that these intoxicating effects were the results of divine possession; certainly the natives came to identify the plant with the supernatural, to feed the holy fires with it and to offer it to their god Manitou, whose spirit was thought to be concealed in rising clouds of smoke. Innumerable religious rites and customs of the Indians sprang from the belief that smoke, through the mystery of fire, disappeared into the void which was held to be the home of the gods, to whom the breath of the pipe was sweet. Smoke, the American natives believed, would calm waters and bring fortune to fishermen; it would protect a warrior and cure a sick child. The pipe of peace was put into the mouth of a bear which had been killed in order to placate its spirit. The Sioux tribe lifted their peace-pipes and said, ' Smoke Sun,' in order to appease the genius of the four elements. Since the Indians believed that tobacco smoke assisted prayer, they showed gratitude to the Great Spirit who bestowed the plant on them so bountifully.

The Indians had different ceremonial pipes for special occasions. The chief of these, the calumet or pipe of peace (see Chapter 4) was the traditional sign of friendship, hospitality and peace. With its use, sometimes in a traditional dance, wars and feuds were brought to a close. Since it was thought to have magical properties, the terms it ratified were inviolable. Thus tobacco, among the Indians, was handed down from the priests to the people and, when the first Europeans arrived in the Americas, the practice of smoking retained much of its sacerdotal character. (Indeed, certain Mexican tribes still blow smoke towards the cardinal points on certain religious occasions.) Immense value was therefore set upon the plant that had the sanction of the priests, that was used by medicine men as a remedial and by laymen as a relief for asthma and catarrh, and which also, in course of time, came to be praised by everyone for the personal pleasures it provided.

§ *From the New World to the Old*

Wherever the early explorers went in the Americas they found different forms of smoking, and they naturally returned to their respective countries with the particular customs they had encountered. In 1492 Columbus was offered dried brown leaves as a friendly gesture. In Cuba, where the practice of chewing tobacco was noted, two members of his crew found natives smoking crudely made cigars; one of these men, Rodrigo de Jerez, who is said to be the first man to smoke tobacco in Europe, was later imprisoned by the Inquisition for this ' devilish ' habit. The monk, Romano Pane, who accompanied Columbus on his second voyage in 1493, reported that the natives of the Antilles used smoke as a remedial and that they sniffed both smoke and powdered tobacco through a Y-shaped hollow stick. This is further confirmed by the Spanish historian, Fernandez de Oviedo who, after many years in the West Indies, published a history in 1526. He wrote:

' Among other evil practices, the Indians have one that is especially harmful, the inhaling of a certain kind of smoke which they call tobacco, in order to produce a state of stupor . . . The caciques (priests) employed a tube, shaped like a Y, inserting the forked extremities in their nostrils and the tube itself in the lighted weed; in this way they would inhale the smoke until they became unconscious and lay sprawling on the earth like men in a drunken slumber. Those who could not procure the right sort of wood took their smoke through a hollow reed ('cañuela'); it is this that the Indians call *tobacco*, and not the weed nor its effects, as some have supposed. They prize this herb very highly, and plant it in their orchards or on their farms for the purpose mentioned above.'

Thus the name which referred originally to the pipe or tube was given by the Spaniards to the plant.

While other explorers, such as Cortez, went on to find snuff and decorated pipes among the immense wealth of the Aztecs, and Cartier found stores of tobacco and pipes among the Indians of Canada (1535-6), the various forms of smoking that were so popular among the sailors began to reach Europe in the ships that plied between America and Spain. Both the plant and the smoking of cigars had reached Spain early in the sixteenth century; a little later smoking was known in Belgium, France and England. But in the greater part of Western Europe, it was its use as a strange and wonderful medicine rather than the pleasures of smoking that brought tobacco almost instantaneous fame.

By 1560, when Portugal's new wealth and imports from across the Atlantic made Lisbon one of the most important westerly ports, the belief that tobacco was an antiseptic and universal remedy for many ailments was firmly established there. While herbalists experimented and the new plants began to appear in the gardens of Portugal and Spain, Jean Nicot, the French ambassador at Lisbon, helped to spread the news that tobacco would cure ulcers and similar complaints and that it was a vital ingredient in all gargles, powders, emetics, inhalations and dentifrices. Though it may be doubted whether the seeds that he sent to Catherine de' Medici, the Queen Mother in France, were the first to produce the 'Holy Plant' on French soil, he encouraged the development of a new era in medical science for which service the botanical name of the plant Nicotiana (and the later 'Nicotine', for the alkaloid in tobacco) remembers him. Monardes in Seville and many other physicians became famous for their cures for bites, headaches, colds, rheumatism and the rest. Fifty years later, in England, the distinguished doctor William Barclay called the plant 'one of the best and surest remedies in the world' for apoplexy and giddiness. Nor is all this surprising in an age when alchemy and astrology and other pseudo sciences were widespread.

It also throws some light on the 'medical whiff' that became a precautionary measure against plague in England, and upon various cures for ulcers, bruises and asthma that lingered on into Victorian days.

¶ *Smoking in England – Elizabethan*

Opinion is still divided about which of the sea captains or colonists in the time of Hawkins and Drake was the first to introduce the plant into the country, and we can only be sure that smoking slowly established itself in England between 1565 and 1590. From the first, however, Englishmen seem to have been more concerned with the pleasures offered by tobacco than with its medical virtues. No doubt the English sailors were the first to become acquainted with cigar and pipe smoking from their rivals in Spanish, Portuguese, French and Flemish ships; some soldiers may have collected tobacco pipes from the Huguenots with whom they fought in France. Smoking was doubtless a familiar practice in the ports of England before the frequently quoted incident of Drake's return from Virginia with a number of colonists in 1586. These men brought with them pipes, tobacco seeds and plants, and their example of what was at first called 'drinking' tobacco smoke (inhaling and apparently swallowing it) is known to have caused considerable excitement and interest. From that time, at any rate, smoking developed from the private pleasure of a few 'tobacconists' – as the first smokers were called – into a social practice.

A tremendous impetus was doubtless given to the habit by the influence and patronage of so distinguished a man as

Sir Walter Raleigh. Every schoolboy knows the story of the servant who found Raleigh smoking and who, thinking that his master was on fire, drenched him with beer. Many fabulous stories have attached themselves to the name of Raleigh who has almost been regarded as the patron saint of smoking; though most of these are probably fictitious and Raleigh was certainly not the first to introduce the plant, he perfected a method of curing the leaf and helped to popularise smoking amongst the courtiers of his day. But smoking was an expensive pleasure; the poor took to it very slowly. Some seventy years later Aubrey wrote in his comments on Raleigh: ' It (tobacco) was sold then for its weight in Silver. I have heard some of our old yeomen neighbours say that when they went to Malmesbury or Chippenham market, they culled out their biggest shillings to lay in the Scales against the Tobacco.' And so, while the Elizabethan dandies with their starched ruffs, gilt-handled swords and velvet breeches, took boxes of silver pipes to the theatre, clay pipes were passed from hand to hand in the so-called ' tabagies ' – meeting-places resembling ordinary taverns. And the poor man had to content himself with a pipe made from a walnut shell and a straw stem.

The contemporary writer, Dekker, employs the term ' artillery ' to describe the elaborate smoking paraphernalia of these fashionable dandies who, especially at the Elizabethan theatre, earned themselves the title of ' reeking gallants'. Such a ' tobacconist ' might carry a set of Winchester clays (or those ornamented with silver and gold), an ivory or metal box which contained up to a pound of tobacco, silver tongs for lifting the glowing ember to light his pipe, a pick, a knife to shred the tobacco and a small scoop for drying the leaf. With such equipment a gallant might sit on a stool at the side of the stage and ' clowding the loathing ayr with foggie fume', as one observer put it, embarrass the actors with his audible criticism. Serving boys supplied lights which were passed from one gallant to another on the point of a sword. It is therefore not surprising that a citizen's wife in a contemporary play should remark, 'This stinking tobacco kills men. Would there were none in England.'

In order to share his pleasure with different company the gallant might direct his steps to St. Paul's – the fashionable resort and meeting-place of sporting men and swaggerers. There, it was said, a man could ' spit private ' and the uninitiated could receive instruction in the solemn ritual of smoking. He could learn to display the fashionable tricks, such as ' The Ring', ' The Whiffe ', ' The Gulp ' and ' The Retention ' – always ' putting the fume through his nose ' – and the bizarre fads which would establish him among the ' reeking gallants ' as an accomplished smoker. From St. Paul's the ' tobacconist ' might wander to a ' tobacco ordinary ', or to the shop of a tobacco-seller – a trade rated almost as low as that of usury – or, turning into the Mermaid Tavern, he might watch the famous writers of the day smoking their pipes with rather less fuss and excitement. Meanwhile Dekker, Marston, Chapman and many others were writing their lampoons on the subject which was already arousing criticism from moralists and clergy. It is therefore simple to imagine the amusement of an audience which heard the water-carrier in Ben Jonson's

The young Heir newly come to his Eftate.
Who very kindly doth invite you all,   To feaſt upon his Fathers funerall.
A new Medly of ſix Ayres.

The Smoking Prodigal: from a wood-cut in *Roxborough's Ballads*, 1620 (*British Museum*)

' Everyman in his Humour ' make the following observation about ' roguish tobacco ':

' It's good for nothing but to choke a man, and fill him full of smoke and embers: there were four died out of one house, last week, with taking of it, and two more the bell went for, yesternight: one of them, they say, will ne'er scape it: he voided a bushel of soot yesterday, upward and downward. By the stocks, and there were no wiser men than I, I'ld have it present whipping, man, or woman, that should but deal with a tobacco pipe: why, it will stifle them all in the end, as many as use it: it's little better than rats-bane (white arsenic) . . . '

Yet, in spite of satire that was bound to make sport of a habit which was taking society by storm, by 1600 smoking ranked in the life of a fashionable man with dancing, riding, hunting and card-playing. It is therefore surprising that there is no direct reference to it in the plays of Shakespeare. He may of course have considered that the subject was already threadbare, or he may have wished to remain *persona grata* at Court. For at the turn of the seventeenth century King James 1st became the centre of the opposition to tobacco which did its utmost to stamp out the ' Indian vice '.

¶ *The Counterblast*

Some pamphleteers insisted that smoking caused sterility and innumerable diseases. Others, supporting the medical virtues of tobacco, thought it illogical to use the weed for pleasure. Indignation at the extravagant smoking habits of the gallants found fulfilment in the famous ' Counterblast to Tobacco' published by James 1st in 1604. This, reflecting much of the King's narrow-mindedness, proclaimed that the habit had been acquired from barbarous people, that ' smoking gallants ' were a social menace, that doctors regarded the habit as dirty and injurious to health, and that to foster the tobacco trade meant playing into the hands of Spanish enemies. The treatise concludes by stating that smoking is . . . ' a custome lothsome to the eye, hatefull to the nose, harmefull to the braine, daungerous to the Lungs, and in the blacke stinking fume thereof, nearest resembling the horrible Stigian smoke of the pit that is bottomelesse.'

In spite of this denunciation from the throne and a subsequent increase in the duty on tobacco (which inevitably encouraged ' bootlegging ', smuggling and the cultivation of the plant on English soil), the popularity of smoking continued. Indeed the consumption of tobacco from Virginia rose to astonishing heights. Whereas, before 1616, the indifferent plant (Nicotiana Rustica) of the English colonies offered little competition to the popular Spanish leaf (Nicotiana Tabacum) which was grown in the West Indies, Mexico and the North of South America, the English colonists, by taking the Spanish plant from Trinidad and planting it in Virginia, began to trade in earnest. Indeed it was largely due to this fact that England kept its hold on North America. In 1616 the first successful shipload of the New Virginian tobacco was sent across the Atlantic. When the colonists asked for women to be sent out to them, their travelling expenses were paid for with tobacco. In 1620 40,000 lbs. of leaf were sent to England where a guild of pipe-makers had been formed, and the increased duties provided a new and immense revenue for the King who had tried to bring this trade to an end. In order to encourage the colonists, even home-grown tobacco, which was making progress around Gloucester and Worcester, was officially prohibited. No wonder that the antiquary Camden, writing in 1625, remarked: 'Tobacco shops are set up in greater numbers than either Alehouses or Tavernes.'

¶ *Persecution*

Meanwhile Portuguese traders, English merchantmen and Dutch mariners had introduced the practice of smoking to every continent in the world except Australia and, by the end of the Thirty Years War (1648), pipe-smoking was known fairly generally throughout Europe. The present outline, however, can only touch briefly on one of the most remarkable chapters in the whole history of the subject – the violent suppressive measures which sprang up in innumerable countries, from Denmark to Japan. In comparison, the opposition to smoking in England was trivial. In Turkey, because smoking was not sanctioned by the Koran, it was thought fit only for the ' Christian dog ' and some offenders, with pipes thrust through their noses, were led on mules through the streets. A Chinese decree of 1638 threatened decapitation to anyone who trafficked in tobacco. Russian offenders were deported to Siberia, and some Czars submitted them to torture and even to death. In parts of Europe the penalties for smoking were less lethal, but many bans were passed, especially by various Popes who threatened offenders with excommunication. Yet it appears that these despotic decrees only encouraged men to smoke in secret, and they began to disappear when rulers realised how tobacco duties could enrich their royal treasuries. Even King James 1st came to recognise the economic value of the plant.

¶ *The Days of Cromwell and the Restoration*

Although King James had considered tobacco ' an abuse and misemployment of the soile of this fruitful kingdome ', many prohibitions against the growth of the plant in England were so unsuccessful that, by 1639, it was being cultivated in about twelve counties. Cromwell appears to have shown some leniency towards the unlawful trade, perhaps because the Royalists were ready to take advantage of the unrest among the persecuted planters. The orders were hard to enforce and the officers sent out by the Privy

An English Interior in the time of the Stuarts: from an engraving in *Sucklington's Faction or Suckling's Roaring Boys*, 1641 (*British Museum*)

Council were sometimes violently resisted. The diary of Pepys shows how the inhabitants of Winchcombe in Gloucestershire ' . . . did not only offer violence but had like to have slaine the sheriff, giving out that they would lose their lives rather than obey the laws in that case provided.'

Meanwhile the holding of a licence to sell tobacco had become obligatory, and as curing methods improved, the trade took up a respectable place alongside that of mercers, tailors and chandlers. Smoking maintained its hold on English peers and squires, parsons and labourers; a few women also enjoyed a pipe of tobacco, if only in the tavern and because the idea that it was good for the health still prevailed. During the Great Plague in 1665, those who kept tobacco shops were supposed not to suffer; those who tended the sick and carted corpses out of the City smoked incessantly, and even boys at Eton were made to smoke in school every morning. When Pepys saw houses marked with the ominous red cross, he was obliged to buy a roll of tobacco to smell and chew. By the end of the seventeenth century, the price of Colonial tobacco had fallen; the Spanish leaf, which had remained popular among the rich, was no longer in great demand and, after further prohibitions, home-grown tobacco had largely disappeared.

¶ *The Eighteenth Century – The Age of Snuff*

Before the beginning of this century, snuff, which had long been popular at the French Court as a more elegant method of taking tobacco, had spread far and wide among fashionable society in western Europe. The etiquette of snuffing, which dominated the whole Augustan Age, is discussed in

Chapter 7, and it is therefore only necessary at this point to record that it was brought to England by the courtiers who returned with Charles 2nd in 1660. Having become a characteristic social practice among fashionable circles by the reign of William and Mary, there appears to have been no outcry when Beau Nash forbad smoking in the public rooms at Bath in 1700. Doubtless the beaux of the period must have thought tobacco pipes somewhat incongruous with their canes, silk handkerchiefs and the combs which they carried for their flowing wigs.

But the snuff-box and the deftly handled pinch did not at first eclipse the pleasure which clergy, squires, merchants and tradesmen continued to find in their clay pipes, whether they used the small, cheap 'Dutch' or the more elegant, long-stemmed Churchwardens. The novels of Fielding and the plates of Hogarth are sufficient to indicate that both in inns and private houses smoking was popular among the professional and working people for the greater part of the century. Even a number of women smoked in privacy. The step-daughter of the Quaker, Charles Fox – to take but one example–made entries in her accounts for tobacco and pipes bought for her mother and sister. Outside fashionable society, the continuing popularity of smoking is indicated by Addison's description of a London coffee-house in 1714:

'I was yesterday in a coffee-house not far from the Royal Exchange, where I observed three persons in close conference over a pipe of tobacco; upon which, having filled one for my own use, I lighted it at the little wax candle that stood before them; and after having thrown in two or three whiffs amongst them, sat down and made one of the company. I need not tell my reader that lighting a man's pipe at the same candle is looked upon among brother-smoakers as an overture to conversation and friendship.'

But this was not the case everywhere, especially in London. Macaulay thus described a more fashionable coffee-house near St. James's Park. 'The atmosphere was like that of a perfumer's shop. Tobacco in any other form than that of richly scented snuff was held in abomination. If any clown, ignorant of the usages of the house, called for a pipe, the sneers of the whole assembly and the short answers of the waiters soon convinced him that he had better go somewhere else. Nor, indeed, would he have had far to go. For, in general, the coffee rooms reeked with tobacco like a guard room, and strangers sometimes expressed their surprise that so many people should leave their own firesides to sit in the midst of eternal fog and stench.'

' Smoking has gone out,' said Dr Johnson in 1773, but this was still not true of the whole of the country. However, he may well have been taking a pinch of snuff from the pocket of his waistcoat as he continued: ' To be sure it is a shocking thing, blowing smoak out of our mouths into other peoples mouths, eyes and noses and having the same thing done to us. Yet I cannot account why a thing which requires so little exertion and yet preserves the mind from total vacuity should have gone out.' Though few could have answered his irony, there were plenty of men who could have shown him that smoking was still practised.

Whether it was smoked or snuffed, increasing supplies of tobacco were required, and in an age of high tariff restric-

A Midnight Modern Conversation: William Hogarth, c.1750 (British Museum)   (facing page 18)

Madame le Brun: Self portrait, 1780

(facing page 19)

tions, tobacco smugglers had elaborate methods for defeating the Government's officials. Illicit traders and bands of armed ruffians smuggled tobacco into the country so that it did not pass through the staple port of London. When, towards the end of the century, a committee was appointed to investigate the position, it was found that: ' Everyone, from pedlar to merchant, seemed possessed with the common desire of defrauding revenue.' It was indeed to be a long time before the King's officers and Excise officials had these practices under effective control.

¶ *The Revival – Smoking in Victorian Days*

During the Napoleonic Wars, the French and British armies fighting in Spain became acquainted with cigar-smoking, and numerous cigars were carried out of that country. These began to appear in England after 1814, and though there was an immediate increase in smoking, the high rate of duty on cigars made them an aristocratic luxury. When the duty was reduced in 1829, many forsook their snuff-boxes for the novelty that was winning increasing popularity, and the new ' smoking-room ' in the House of Commons helped to spread the fashion. But, as in earlier days, smoking still had its opponents. Queen Victoria hated it in all its forms; the Duke of Wellington issued orders to restrain smoking in the Army. Moralists once more took to their pens. Feminine society professed to shun those who ' reeked of the weed.' Although in some early Victorian households men had to take themselves away from the ladies and smoke surreptitiously up the chimney or in the stables, the vogue for cigars steadily increased and was gradually sanctioned in London clubs. The practice spread less rapidly in some European capitals; in Berlin, for example, official orders prohibiting smoking in public were not withdrawn until the middle of the 19th century.

At this point the Cigarette makes a dramatic entry into the story. Aboriginal Mexican ' smoke tubes ' – reeds filled with a tobacco mixture – had been seen by Spanish ex-plorers in the sixteenth century. There was therefore nothing essentially new about the diminutive, dainty, paper-covered cigar which bewitched England and France in the 1850's and whose popularity spread a little later to the United States. From Spain, where various types of wrapper had been tried for small cigars and paper had been popular as early as the seventeenth century, these ' pepe-letes ', as they were called, had spread eastwards to Turkey and Russia. Thus, during the Crimean War (1854-56) they were introduced to English and French troops, and their immediate success helped to bring about the revival in smoking that had been started by cigars. Though the officers who introduced the novelty into London clubs (together with the fashion for wearing beards) and the men who first smoked cigarettes in the streets were laughed at, they had brought home the form of smoking that was to win unpre-cedented popularity. Since it was less expensive to roll one's own cigarettes than to buy ready-made cigars, the new demand increased and it resulted almost immediately in improved cigarettes, machinery and rapid methods of pro-duction.

In the second half of the Victorian era, when so many conventions within the rigid social order were beginning to be challenged, smoking played an important minor role. There was a pamphlet war by reformers who would have banished the tobacco habit for ever; public opinion proclaimed the vulgarity of smoking in public places such as Hyde Park for the rest of the century. While moralists could continue to be horrified at ' sly cigarettes between feminine lips at croquet parties ', smoking in the presence of ladies remained a social crime. Even after 1868, when separate smoking-compartments on trains were introduced, a gentleman was not permitted to take into the ' smoking-room ' of his London club the precious meerschaum pipe which, if he was lucky enough to have his own ' smoking-room ', he might have enjoyed in privacy. Nor was the ' wooden pipe ' – the Briar – which won wide popularity among pipe-smokers during the last quarter of the century, permitted in fashionable clubs; there, where gentlemen smoked cigars and perhaps cigarettes, even the snuff-box, that had been so popular a hundred years earlier, stood neglected on the mantlepiece.

Meanwhile most public houses had their trade in Churchwardens and Broseley clays, and encouraged the smoking and hiring of them by keeping a tobacco-box on the table. When a smoker had inserted a penny or halfpenny, he was trusted by the landlord to take no more than a fill for his pipe and to close the lid of the box. The pipes were cleaned by heat from the fire and iron holders were kept on the hearth for this purpose. The glowing coal or smouldering charcoal continued to be a simple method for lighting the pipe, but a tinder-box might have been seen on the shelf in any public-house until about the middle of the

century; thereafter a large variety of matches, from Lucifers and Congreves to Vestas and Safeties, strove for popularity. (See Chapter 8).

¶ *The Twentieth Century*
By 1908 one eighth of the tobacco smoked in England was
in the form of cigarettes. Some Edwardian gentlemen preferred hand-made Turkish cigarettes which they smoked
through amber holders and carried in fine cases, but the
majority still smoked cigars, ornamented meerschaum
pipes or one of the new Briars. By 1914, however, when
half the total amount of leaf imported into Britain was
made into cigarettes, it was apparent that this, the most
compact and simple form of smoking possible, was to tri-
umph over every other. During the First World War
smoking, especially cigarettes, increased still further. The
Commander in Chief of American troops cabled to Wash-
ington: ' Tobacco is as indispensable as the daily ration: we
must have thousands of tons of it without delay.' In the
years between the World Wars the British and American
consumption of tobacco increased steadily as smoking became an integral part of peoples' lives. To-day most of the
conventional bans on smoking have been relaxed, but there
are still a few places and occasions in which pipe-smoking
is discouraged although cigars and cigarettes are allowed.
Anomalies such as these, which usually have their explana-
tion linked with the Victorian past, still survive. But the
cigarette, which is perhaps as characteristic of this century
as snuff was of the eighteenth, has persistently increased its
hold on every part of modern society. Nor is this surpris-

ing. Cigarettes are light, compact, easily lit and suitable for all occasions. To-day cigarettes consume four-fifths of the total supply of leaf to the United Kingdom.

Who can foretell the future? To-day, when prices and taxes in Britain restrict the choice which smokers might otherwise make, and impose a serious handicap on the whole tobacco trade, cigarettes remain incomparably the most popular form of smoking everywhere. Nevertheless, this may not always be so. Though pipe-smokers are in the minority, most of them are passionately devoted to their choice and a large variety of pipes are in constant demand. Even a few women are once again turning their attention to pipe-smoking. And again, though comparatively few Britons smoke choice imported cigars except on special occasions, high prices alone can account for this fact; in the United States where prices are lower, cigars remain popular. During the last decade, in certain districts in Britain, the popularity of snuff has increased considerably, if only for reasons of economy. Will it again become the vogue which it was in the eighteenth century?

As we have seen, the ways in which tobacco is enjoyed must vary from country to country and from time to time. Doubtless it will continue so, and only one prophecy seems safe. Whatever the future may hold, man is unlikely to forsake the plant whose pleasures have enchanted him for so long.

CHAPTER II

THE GROWING OF TOBACCO

'Of all the weeds grown on earth, sure the nicotian is the most soothing and salutary.'

THACKERAY *Esmond*

¶ *The Plant*

The family of plants called Solanaceae, of which tobacco is a member, contains some 1,800 species, including garden pepper, deadly nightshade, petunias and the Irish potato. Tobacco belongs to the genus Nicotiana which grows in various forms in different parts of the world; about thirty species (rather more than half the total number) are used to decorate gardens in England; two derive from China and two from Australia. But the species Nicotiana Tabacum, or Common Tobacco, which is considered to be native to central America and the north of South America and which was introduced into Europe about 1530, is now grown all over the world and provides about three-quarters of the tobacco that is smoked. The number and size of the leaves vary, but a single leaf can measure 24 ins. by 18, so that a plant such as those used for cigar tobacco may have 18 leaves which have a total area of 25 square feet. It is therefore a large wide-spreading plant, growing to a height of six or seven feet. But its habit-forming properties when smoked – properties which are largely due to the content of nicotine – are shared with other species of Nicotiana.

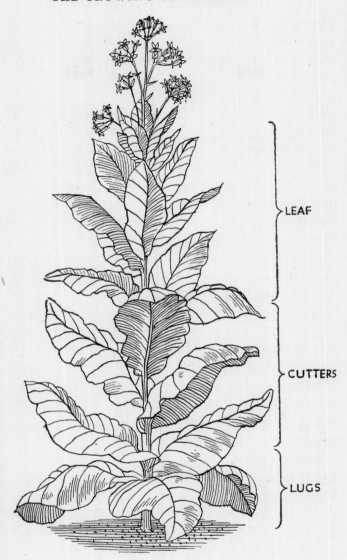

The Tobacco Plant

The particular popularity of Nicotiana Tabacum for commercial production is therefore due to its habits of growth, its aroma and the many other smoking qualities of the cured leaf.

To the ordinary smoker only two other species of tobacco are important. The first is a smaller plant with a white flower which is found in Persia and is sometimes seen in English gardens. This Nicotiana Persica produces a mild tobacco known as Shiraz. The second, Nicotiana Rustica, is a hardier plant than Nicotiana Tabacum and grows with greenish brown leaves and a pale yellowish flower to a height of three or four feet. It is now cultivated chiefly in Europe, Asia and Africa, but it is this plant which originally grew in Virginia until the Virginia Company imported the more popular Spanish variety (Nicotiana Tabacum) from Trinidad and thus brought prosperity to their trade at a critical time. The leaves of Nicotiana Rustica are also milder than those of Nicotiana Tabacum and are important because they produce Turkish, Syrian and Latakia tobaccos – popular ingredients in many smoking mixtures. Most smokers are familiar with the dark fragments of Latakia – a leaf that is cured by the heat and fumes from the wood of the Asiatic oak.

Nicotiana Tabacum, with which the smoker is principally concerned, has a bright bluish-green leaf which lightens to a yellowish green as it reaches maturity. In its natural state it is bitter to taste and even when it has been cured, or dried slowly, so that the leaves become yellow and orange in colour, it still does not produce a smooth, mellow smoke. Not until the dried leaf has had a period of

fermentation or ageing can it provide the rich, fresh
smoking qualities for which it is famous. The tobacco produced by most amateurs falls far short of professional stan-
dards through lack of fermentation and, more particularly,
because it has been incorrectly and inadequately cured. In
small quantities the plant is not difficult to grow, but, as
later paragraphs of this chapter will show, curing by one of
various methods is a highly skilled and crucial stage in
tobacco production; only when this has been carried out
carefully, and the long natural process of fermentation has
radically changed the composition of the leaf, will it produce the mellow, rich smoke that is required.

¶ *The Cultivation of Tobacco*

In a temperate climate, between 40 and 50 degrees latitude,
the plant flourishes in a suitable soil with good drainage.
Yet it is grown as far north as Sweden and as far south as
New Zealand. North America, Mexico and the West Indies,
however, produce about a quarter of the world's supplies,
and Asia about one half. But British manufacturers are
making an increasing use of Empire tobaccos, especially
the Flue-cured leaf of Rhodesia, Canada and India. In 1951,
for example, when 200 million lbs. of tobacco were imported from U.S.A., 50 million lbs. of Rhodesian leaf were
also received into Britain.

Soil, climate and prevailing conditions are different in
every plantation and an average yield of 1,100 lbs. of
tobacco per acre, which is accurate for some areas in the
United States, is only an approximate guide for other parts
of the world. The cultivation of tobacco requires constant

Tobacco Seed Beds

care and experienced attention because every soil has different effects on the plant, and the minerals in the earth, which form the ash of burning tobacco, are rapidly exhausted. About four lbs. of burnt tobacco produce one lb. of ash or mineral matter, so that the ground requires constant manuring and treatment with potash and nitrogen. In some areas a rotation of crops may be required, but in all cases the processes of fertilization are scientific and vary from soil to soil.

Because the seed is so small – about three hundred thousand make up an ounce, which is enough for 200 square yards of seed-bed – direct sowing in the field is not practicable; seedlings must be developed in cold frames or hot beds until they reach the size required for transplanting. Sowing in these beds, which are carefully nourished, drained, protected from the sun and ventilated, may take place in the United States from December to May. In about six to ten weeks the plants are ready for transplanting which, depending on the latitude, takes place from March to June. The harvest in June or July may be as late as August in some northern states.

In the spring, the fields of a plantation are prepared in one of two ways. They are either hoed into shallow trenches two or three feet apart, with ridges between them, or they may be left flat so that the plants can be set out in squares. The important point, as with most forms of planting, is to maintain a constant number of plants in each acre, because any variation may have a serious effect on the size and quality of the leaves. The planting is done by hand or with the assistance of a simple machine which waters, opens and closes the furrow for the hand-planter. Some 4,000 – 10,000 plants may be put into each acre and each plant may produce a quarter of a pound of tobacco.

If the plants escape the many dangers which surround them – even on ground that is carefully prepared and completely free from weeds – they grow rapidly. The leaves nearest the ground, which have first call on the sap, are the strongest, while those at the top are the mildest. Hence, by constant attention and pruning, a planter can control the strength of his crop. By breaking out the terminal bud (' topping ') the size of the leaves can be increased, but this may not be necessary if a thin, light-coloured leaf is required. Suckers and side-shoots are nipped off so that the plant concentrates on its principal leaves. Pruning and priming may include the picking of certain leaves before the rest have reached maturity.

In spite of constant watchfulness and attention, a single night's frost may destroy a whole crop; even when the plants are reaching maturity, disasters can be caused by wet weather. This can produce a blight known as ' firing ', and extreme heat and drought can infect the leaves with hard brown spots which perforate and destroy them. (Plants for cigar wrapper tobacco, for example, must have cloth or sash covers to protect them from the sun.) Some twelve diseases are responsible for the loss of about 15% of the total yield in the United States. Bacteria or a fungus, such as ' Blackshank ', can attack the plant and cause the wilting of a whole field; others attack the root and even cause damage during curing. Moreover, in spite of the fact that nicotine is an insecticide, there are numerous insects such as Hornworm and Wireworm which can cause considerable destruction.

¶ Harvesting

Two distinct methods are used. In the first, the stalk is cut above the ground by a special type of hatchet or shears and, when the leaves have wilted in the sun, the whole plant is taken to a curing barn. By the second method, the leaves are picked or primed as they mature. This begins at the bottom of the plant and takes two to five leaves at each picking. Although the second method involves more labour, each leaf is harvested at its proper stage of maturity; the total crop may be increased because the leaves remaining on the stalk are stimulated after each successive picking. By the first method, the plants are normally prepared for curing in the field. The butt of the stalk is pierced and five to eight plants are strung on to a lath; these laths are collected and carried to the curing plant in waggons. Burley, a widely grown American leaf, is cured on the stalk in this way. By the second method, however, the separate leaves are usually packed into canvas lined boxes and taken to the curing plant where they are strung for curing in a similar fashion.

§ *Curing*

Leaves that are simply dried have little more odour or taste than any other dried leaf. It is the curing and fermentation that gives the leaf its particular flavour. In all methods of curing the leaves may be partly dried by the sun, but the two principal processes thereafter are known as Air-Curing and Flue-Curing. In the first, the leaves are allowed to hang on their laths in large well-ventilated barns under natural conditions, although some artificial heat may be used in wet weather. Flue-cured tobacco is put into smaller barns which are heated by pipes or flues to temperatures which vary from 90 to 170 degrees F. Careful adjustments to the temperature are required throughout, especially when the leaf has turned yellow; if it is dried too slowly, it turns dark and loses its correct aroma and taste. It is the Flue-curing that gives the leaf a bright, golden colour. In addition to these methods smoke from hard wood and sawdust may be used, but in all cases the main point is to bring the leaf to the right colour and to effect the necessary chemical changes.

Leaves on tier poles in the barn

The fresh leaf that goes to the barn for curing contains about 80% moisture so that, in order to obtain 1,000 lbs. of cured leaf, about 5,000 lbs. of fresh leaf will be necessary and about two tons of water will be lost during the process of curing.

¶ Grading

After curing in these barns the crop is graded. This is a complex, technical business which varies from one plantation to another and which depends on the methods of harvesting, curing and the type of leaf in question. In 'Cigar-filler' districts, for example, the leaf is divided into two major grades and a minor one known as ' trash ' which has little commercial value. In plants of the ' flue-cured ' type, however, the separate primings simplify the process of grading. The lower part of the plant, which ripens first, is called ' lugs ', and the upper, thicker and more oily part provides the 'leaf'.* Both are further divided into sub grades. The leaves just above the ' lugs ' are known as ' cutters ' because they are especially suitable for cutting and shredding into cigarette tobacco. In unusually fine ' flue-cured ' crops, a few ' cutters ' may be suitable as ' wrappers ' – the out-side leaves which surround plug tobaccos. Such leaves must be strong, elastic, free from injury and have only small veins. They are normally specially grown under shade.

When, according to the type of plant and the prevailing conditions, the crop has been graded, the leaves of each grade are tied into bunches called ' hands '. The butts of 10 to 15 leaves in the best grades are tied by another leaf, and these ' hands ' are collected and stacked on the warehouse floor at the plantation, or packed into boxes or hogsheads.

§ *Fermentation*

The term ' curing ' properly refers to this regulated drying of the freshly harvested leaf in the curing-barn on the farm; this is a living process involving the loss of water and the green colour of the leaf. The further process of fermen-tation, or ageing, begins as soon as the ' hands ' are stacked on the warehouse floor and continues until the hogsheads, in which they are finally packed under hydraulic pressure, are opened by the manufacturer at his factory. This natural process of ' sweating ', which varies with the type of pack-

* *See page 25*

ing used and the seasonal changes in temperature, makes the leaf undergo a radical change which has a fundamental effect on its quality as tobacco. The fermentation may take from six to 12 months with some types of leaf, and from 18 months to three years with others. Too short a period may fail to produce the full aroma and taste, and too long a period may spoil them. The methods of controlling this difficult process depend on the amount of moisture in the particular leaf, how tightly it is packed and where it is grown and stored.

¶ *Marketing*

Although, in the case of Cigar leaf, dealers still make individual contracts with farmers at their plantations, and some farmers in the United States still send packed hogsheads to market for auction, the bulk of tobacco throughout the world to-day is bought and sold by the Loose Leaf Auction system. In the United States and Africa, for example, there are warehouses which employ this system reasonably close to most plantations so that the tobacco does not deteriorate through the delay of a long journey. Since, by this method, all leaf is spread out in baskets on the warehouse floor and marked by cards which indicate its weight and grade, every buyer can see it and is not dependant on samples, and every seller can compare his price with that of similar grades and with the guiding price quoted by government officials.

The auctioneering procedure at such markets is puzzling to the stranger if only because some 400 to 600 baskets are sold in a single hour; the appropriate transactions are completed with the auctioneer and his staff, and all the tobacco in the warehouse is sold, taken away and replaced at re-markable speed. Immense quantities of harvested tobacco have to be sold during a comparatively short season if the leaf is to avoid deterioration. By this system, although all the leaf is inspected, no time is wasted.

After the auction purchase, the brokers who are con-cerned with export take the leaf to their warehouses, arrange for its mechanical re-drying and conditioning, and pack the grades required by particular manufacturers into hogsheads or bales. Leaf for the United Kingdom is shipped to such ports as Liverpool, Glasgow, Bristol and London where it is weighed by the Excise authorities.

CHAPTER III

THE PREPARATION OF TOBACCO FOR SMOKING

' For thy sake, tobacco, I
Would do anything but die.'
CHARLES LAMB   *A Farewell to Tobacco*

¶ *Tobacco Duties*

In countries such as Britain which prepare imported leaf, the tobacco is taken from the ports and stored in bonded warehouses. If required, the Warehouse authorities, under Customs' supervision, send samples to the manufacturers or importers. In normal economic conditions, two or three years elapse before the tobacco is withdrawn, and then manufacturers draw on this bonded stock by the simple expedient of paying the appropriate duty on the weight of the tobacco when it was landed at the port. If the leaf was particularly dry, extra duty must be paid. Moreover, it is increasingly necessary for British manufacturers to make the utmost use of every part of the leaf they buy, for, unless the circumstances are exceptional, only 6% of their total consignment may be returned as ' drawback ' – the surplus scrap and stem on which the Excise authorities will refund the duty. This ' drawback ' is later resold for the making of insecticides and similar commodities.

Most people in the United Kingdom and Empire

probably realise the immense sums which the Exchequer obtains in this way. In the first half of this century the duty on tobacco has risen from 3s to approximately 58s per pound (the duty payable on Empire grown tobacco being at present about 1s 6d per pound less). Thus, in the price of the modern packet of 20 cigarettes, about 2s 10d is spent in paying duty. The total annual revenue produced for the British Exchequer by tobacco taxation is approximately £600 million.

In the United States, where taxes vary from state to state, the average tax on one pound of smoking tobacco has risen in fifty years from 8.7 to 23.5 cents. To-day taxes range from 40 – 60% of the cost of a package of cigarettes, so that Federal, State and Municipal taxes account for approximately 10 cents in a package costing 25 cents.

¶ Unpacking the Tobacco

When the leaf is unpacked from the hogsheads at the factory, it contains about 10 – 15% moisture, and considerably more is required during various stages of manufacture. But if packed cigarettes and most types of tobacco for pipe-smoking left the factory with a high moisture content, they would soon deteriorate in storage. Only a few types of tobacco, such as ' Twist ', are in fact packed with the maximum moisture content of 32% which is permitted by British law. Tobacco manufacture therefore includes a cycle of drying and humidifying.

Partly on account of higher temperatures, tobacco is prepared somewhat differently in the United States. Some hygroscopic substance, which must be combustible and odourless, is used to increase the moisture-holding properties of the leaf. Diethylene glycol is now replacing the use of glycerine for this purpose, and manufacturers prepare their leaf with various forms of sugar, including glucose and molasses; they also give an attractive smell to the finished product by spraying it with a preparation that may contain licorice or sugar. Such preparations, however, are not permitted by British law.

In order to separate the ' hands ' that were tightly packed under hydraulic pressure in the country of their origin, the hogsheads, clearly labelled with weight, grade and type of cured leaf, are stored for about a week in the maximum temperature and humidity that is not injurious to the tobacco. The ' hands ' can then be taken out without risk of damage; they are then loosened and piled in such a way that the air can circulate through them.

The Leaf Room

Stemming Tobacco

❡ *Stemming*

They are prepared for ' stemming ' – the removal of the thick, woody midrib or stem – by the addition of moisture from steam-heated ovens or by Casing machines. In the latter the leaf is passed through a steam chamber and rotating drum in which it is moistened by fine jets of water or steam. Tobacco which is thus raised to a moisture content of about 18% – too much steam will darken it – is said to be ' in case ', and is then ready for stemming.

There are various types of machine that remove the stem from the leaf automatically, and some perform this operation more cleanly than others. Indeed many manufacturers still find that stemming by hand produces work of a higher

39

quality than any other method. Whatever method is used, the stems may later be rolled or crushed flat and reintroduced into the blend either before or after it has been cut. And if as in the United States, a 'casing preparation' is used, this will be added before the stemmed leaf is ready for the Cigarette machines.

¶ *Blending*

Since some leaf has more aroma and strength than others and all have different burning qualities, blending is one of the most important features of manufacture. One type of leaf strengthens the deficiencies of another, so that the combination of two or more types will normally produce a more satisfactory tobacco for smoking. It does not follow in the making of cigars, for example, that a 'binder', 'filler' and 'wrapper' from the same leaf of first quality will make a perfect Havana; in fact they do not. Different types of leaf have to be matched and blended. This process is also important because crops vary seasonally and from place to place; by slight variations in the proportions of leaf that is available, manufacturers are able to blend and maintain a supply of popular brands whose principal characteristics remain constant.

Some of the blending is carried out after the various grades of leaf have been cut. In the manufacture of some cigarettes, leaf may be taken from as many as twenty different grades, and this is mixed roughly on a conveyor belt which carries it forward to the next stage. Details in the process must vary, however, with the type of leaf that a manufacturer is using at any particular time.

¶ *The Cutting and Drying of Tobacco for Cigarettes*

The latest type of Cutting machine feeds the tobacco through rollers which compress it into a compact mass known as ' cheese '. When it has passed through a hardened steel throat, it is met by a series of knives on a rotary cutter; these are fastened like the blades of a fan and are automatically ground and adjusted as they wear down. With 50 to 60 cuts to the inch, these knives shave the leaf into long strands a little less than a millimeter wide. Some factories, however, still use high speed vertical cutters with heavy steel blades that have to be sharpened about every eight minutes.

The leaf is then passed to a Drying machine which consists of steam or gas-heated rotating drums with internal spikes which tease the tobacco as the drums revolve. Although they still contain a high degree of moisture, the strands are unfolded and considerably lengthened during the process. In the Cooling machine which follows, a fan sucks out the moist air, and rotating mesh drums sift away the dust and the sand that stick especially to the lower leaves of the plant. The tobacco then passes over a magnetised drum, outside the machine, which extracts any particles of metal, nails or scraps of wire that may have fallen into the leaf when the hogsheads were opened.

The prepared 'filler' or 'rag', as the cigarette leaf is called at this stage, is usually stored for one or two days so that, when it is delivered to the Cigarette Machines, it will be light and fluffy.

¶ *The Cigarette Machine*

In order to meet the demands of to-day, factories are equipped with machines capable of producing 1,000–1,500 cigarettes per minute. The speed at which these machines are fed is of fundamental importance because this will determine the weight of the individual cigarette. The 'rag' is carried forward from the hopper by spikes, and as it passes along, any uncrushed pieces of stem that still remain are extracted. A fine, uniform stream of tobacco is thus delivered through a chute on to the paper.

Before receiving the tobacco, the paper is fed from a reel in a continuous strip. It passes a revolving die which prints the brand-name and name of the manufacturer at appropriate intervals. If cork-tipped cigarettes are being made, the machine also carries a reel of wafer-thin natural cork which is cut and pasted automatically on to the paper at regular intervals.

As the tobacco is fed on to the paper, it is shaped by compression rollers; one edge of the paper is turned up by a tongue piece and a line of pure casein adhesive is supplied by a wheel. The paper is then folded around the tobacco and, in the form of a long, continous rod, both pass through an electrically heated chamber where the adhesive is dried. Cigarettes with filter tips, however, need to be treated differently and are made on a special machine.

The thin blades of the rotary cutters, which sharpen themselves on an emery wheel, cut this rod into individual cigarettes. An automatic weighing-machine may gather up 10% of the total output – taking about 100 cigarettes every minute; if these vary fractionally from the standard weight, the amount is recorded by a scale and the speed of tobacco supply is adjusted automatically. Thus, as the finished

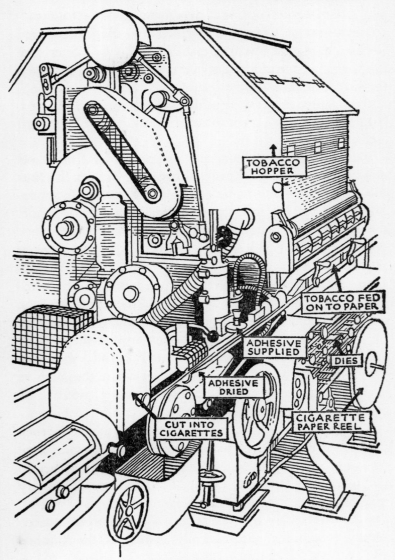

The Cigarette Machine: the parts illustrated

cigarettes appear almost faster than the eye can follow, they are fed into trays. Each tray, as it is removed from the machine, is inspected by eye, and any cigarettes that are not perfectly pasted, lapped, printed or filled are immediately discarded. The imperfect cigarettes go to the Ripping Machine which separates the paper from the tobacco so that the latter may be used again.

After a final inspection and before packing, the cigarettes may go for twenty-four hours to a Conditioning Room where hot air reduces the moisture to the amount suitable for smoking.

¶ *Packing*

The machines in this department of the factory are equally ingenious. From the feeding hopper 10 or 20 cigarettes are automatically fed on to the ' slide ' or inside portion of the carton. Platinum pointed screws feel and ' count ' the cigarettes on the ' slide ' and, through a system of electrical relays, a bell is rung if the incorrect number of cigarettes is passed on to the main track of the machine. The defective packet can then be identified and the mistake corrected. A separate magazine holds the ' shells ' or outside portions of the cartons and, as these move forward, the ' slides ' are automatically inserted into them. With only one or two attendants to assist it, the Packing Machine is therefore able to ' count ' the cigarettes, to fill, close and, if necessary, label the carton and to do all this in perfect synchronisation at the rate of 120 cartons per minute.

After inspection, the cartons may be passed to a Cellophane Wrapper which can fold and seal the wrapping with

The Cigarette Machine: (*above*) a general view (*below*) a view showing the rod passing to the cutters

(*facing page 44*)

remarkable speed. These may then be put into larger cartons, or made into parcels by a machine which folds the paper automatically and sticks it into position by pressure and heat.

¶ *Cigarettes in General*

Any account of cigarette manufacture must emphasise the fact that the whole process is subject to continual supervision by engineers and chemists whose work ranges from the installation and operation of this elaborate machinery to the constant checking of moisture content and the analysis and control of adhesives and papers. Moreover, variations in methods and plants produce a great variety of cigarettes, and many smokers are unaware of the great choice that is offered them. There are innumerable types and grades between the expensive hand-filled cigarettes and the popular ' Virginian ', whose name no longer implies that its tobacco comes only from Virginia. Many kinds of leaf, including Turkish, may be used in the preparation of so-called Virginian cigarettes. British factories also make blended cigarettes of the American type as well as Turkish and Egyptian; these are of course distinct from the cigarettes which are imported ready-made from such countries. There are also a few distinctive types such as Cyprus, Brazilian, Algerian, Mexican, Havana and Russian.

¶ *Pipe Tobaccos*

The unpacking and preliminary preparation of the leaf is, in the main, similar to that of cigarette tobacco. But since pipe tobaccos differ considerably in their smoking qualities and characteristics and since some of them are still made by the traditional methods of a few manufacturers, the final stages of production vary with the particular leaf, brand and factory in question. Blending may occur in the Leaf Room or after the tobacco has been cut; some brands require both stages. Although the majority of leaf is stemmed, the stem, at some stage or another, may form an important ingredient in the final blend. All the stem of the dark fire-cured Latakia, for example, is used; Indian leaf, on the other hand, is stemmed before it reaches the British factory. And it is interesting to note that machinery has not wholly standardised the methods of making pipe tobaccos. The manufacturer, like the tobacconist who blends ' Mixtures ' to suit the requirements of individual smokers, has methods which satisfy the particular market he supplies.

¶ The Principal Types

Popular pipe tobaccos in the factory may be considered in three main groups. The first, which includes 'Flakes', 'Plug' and ' Bar Tobacco ', is made from leaf that is pressed into a cake. The leaf for such tobaccos as ' Twist ' and ' Spun Cut ', in the second group, is made initially into the form of a rope. And the third group, which includes ' Shags ', many plain ' Virginias ' and ingredients used in the blending of ' Mixtures ', is made from unpressed tobacco which is cut into shreds by a guillotine type of cutting machine.

The exact price of a particular brand must depend on various factors, especially on the quality of the leaf used in any particular part of the blend. Some tobaccos naturally involve more complex processes than others, and before

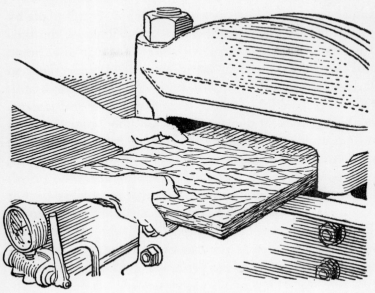

Pressing Flake

giving an account of some of the differences between the various types, it is convenient to outline the manufacture of 'Flake' since this gives a general idea of the whole process by which pipe tobaccos are made.

¶ *The Manufacture of 'Flake', 'Navy Cut' and 'Plug' Tobaccos*
When the leaf has been prepared, stemmed and mixed by hand, it is put into moulding presses and, under hydraulic pressure of about $1\frac{1}{2}$ tons per square inch, it is pressed into 'cakes'. These are put into retaining presses which, according to the nature and colour of the tobacco required, may be either cold or heated by steam-jackets. The amount

47

of pressure and the amount of 'stoving' by heat will determine the final colour of the blend. When a Splitting Machine has cut the pressed 'cakes' into sticks of the required width, these are then passed through a guillotine type of cutting machine which cuts them into slices or flakes.

'Flake' can be recognised by these characteristic slices, though a few 'Cut Cakes' and partly unravelled 'Flakes' are on the market, and a few are ready-rubbed for the pipe. 'Plug' and 'Bar' tobacco is also made by moulding the leaf under pressure. Similar also is the preparation of 'Straight Cuts', though this term meant originally that the cut has been made down the length of the leaf. To-day, however, various terms connected with pipe tobaccos are, if not redundant, little more than an echo of the past. 'Virginia' no longer implies that its tobacco comes only from Virginia. 'Navy Cut' is an interesting survival which refers to the days when sailors formed their own duty-free leaf into the shape of a cigar, covered it with canvas and bound it tightly with a cord. The solid plug of tobacco which resulted was shredded and rubbed by hand. But to-day, 'Navy Cut' is made in a way similar to that of any other 'Flake'. The term 'Birds-eye', however, still refers appropriately to the small cross-sections of stem that can be seen in this and some other types of tobacco.

When finished and packed these blends leave the factory with a moisture content of 20% and upwards.

¶ *'Roll', 'Twist', 'Negrohead' and 'Spun Cut'*.
A different sequence of processes is necessary for these brands. The leaf that may be used as 'filler' is rolled inside

a ' wrapper ' leaf, and the whole is spun by machine into the form of a continuous rope which may be from one eighth to about one and a quarter inches thick. In the case of ' Roll ' and ' Twist ', oil is applied to the outside of the rope during spinning so that, when coiled and wrapped in canvas, the coils of tobacco do not stick together. Both brands, when spun, are wrapped in canvas, tightly corded and put into steam-heated presses under heavy pressure for several weeks. When the rich, black ' Twist ' is mature, it is either sent to the retailer in rolls of various sizes or is cut into short lengths and wrapped. When the ropes of ' Roll ' or ' Twist ' are plaited together, the tobacco is given the time-honoured name of ' Negrohead '.

' Curly Cut ' and ' Spun Cut ', when made with the best quality leaf, are lighter in appearance and are relatively expensive. By a similar process the dark and light leaf which makes the ' filler ' are put into a ' wrapper ' formed from a light flue-cured leaf and, when the whole has been spun by machine, the rope of tobacco is cut into discs. One of these small circles, a cross-section of the original rope, reveals the various types of leaf that have been used.

¶ ' *Shags* ', ' *Plain Virginias* ' and ' *Mixtures* '.
' Shag ' tobaccos, which may be light or dark in colour, are not made from ' cakes '. The leaf is cut very fine and it undergoes a thorough ' panning ' by hand. Gas or steam-heated pans remove some of the moisture and open out the tobacco into its characteristic long strands. It is then formed into ' cobs ' or small bundles which are allowed to stand for 24 hours. A few British brands of ' Shag ' are scented;

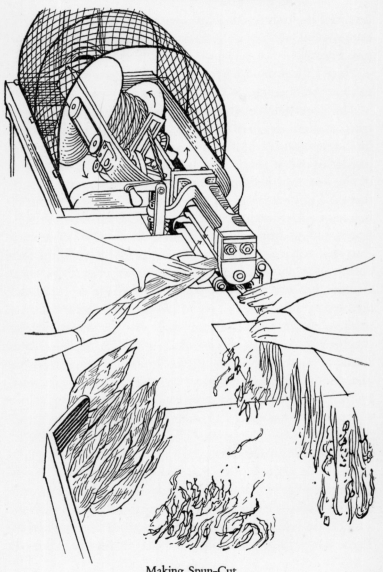

Making Spun-Cut

artificial flavourings, however, are seldom admired by the connoisseur and are not often to be found in more expensive brands.

Plain ' Virginia ' tobaccos are similarly prepared, though they are seldom cut as fine as ' Shag '.

The popularity of the many brands and types of ' Mixture ' should set them in a class apart – and a class which includes some of the finest pipe tobaccos obtainable. The essence of every good ' Mixture ' lies not only in the quality of the leaf, but in the final blending of the various ingredients. Kentucky leaf in the United States or, as in the better quality blends of Britain, Virginia leaf may form the body, and to this may be added Turkish leaf, some dark ' stoved ' tobacco, some ' unstoved ' tobacco to lighten the colour and some Latakia to give it a fuller flavour. In Britain, Empire tobaccos, particularly those of Rhodesia, are used in the making of some ' Mixtures ', and in addition to the dark ' stoved ' tobacco and Latakia, which counteracts the hot-burning effects of the lighter leaf, there may be added a small quantity of Perique whose influence on the blend may be compared with the use of pepper as a spice. Finally the appropriate quantities of the various ingredients are mixed thoroughly in a blending drum.

¶ *American Pipe Tobaccos*
The custom in the United States of increasing the moisture-holding properties of the leaf and of flavouring it after blending with various forms of sugar, glucose and molasses has already been emphasised in connection with cigarettes. These flavourings are equally popular in pipe tobaccos. In

other respects, American brands, such as ' Plug Cut ' and ' Mixtures ' are similar to British; the majority are blended, but a few are made from Burley leaf.

Granulated tobacco is so popular that it deserves to be mentioned separately. The lug-grades of flue-cured tobacco (see page 31) and various blends including Burley leaf are stemmed and moistened; the granulating, which used to be carried out by beating the leaf with sticks, is today performed by machines. It is afterwards treated with such flavourings as the tonka bean and is often packed in small cotton bags.

Various types of processed tobacco are used both for smoking and chewing. The 'Black Fat', for example, which is exported to Africa, is prepared by treating the leaf with mineral fat, and then subjecting it to heat and pressure until it is changed into a black, oily, leathery product. Such tobaccos have a relatively high moisture content – a tendency which applies to many American brands.

CHAPTER IV

A SHORT HISTORY OF PIPES

' A Pipe! It is a great soother, a pleasant comforter. Blue devils fly before its honest breath. It ripens the brain, it opens the heart; and the man who smokes thinks like a sage and acts like a Samaritan.'

BULWER LYTTON

¶ *Makeshift Pipes*

The making of a pipe by hand, even with the best materials, is no simple feat: the bowl must be carved and hollowed, the stem bored and fitted, and the mouthpiece shaped smoothly to the lips. It is therefore not surprising that primitive savages should have set so much value on pipes that were often made from inadequate materials and with the utmost ingenuity. The Monbuttu, for example, who live on a tributary of the Congo, discovered centuries ago how to make a pipe by boring the midrib of a plantain leaf and inserting into a small opening in this stem the leaf itself, twisted up into a cornet and filled with tobacco.* The Eskimo, in the snow wastes of North America, is also naturally short of material, and the makeshift pipe that has there been popular is made by scooping out the end of a willow twig, splitting the stem, removing the pith, and binding the two halves together with a raw hide thong. Similar pipes have been popular among Chinese coolies and in tropical

* *See next page*

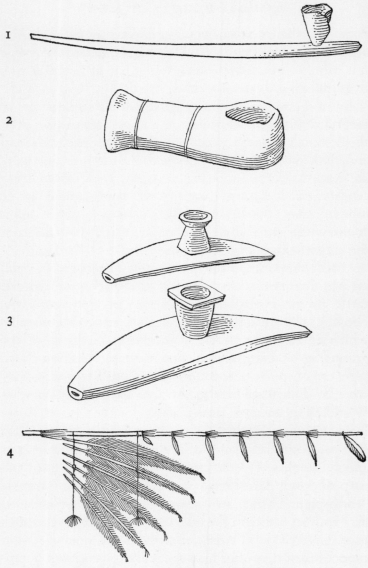

(1) Monbuttu Plantain Leaf Pipe (2) South African Hottentot
Earth Pipe (3) Two American Indian Mound Pipes (4) Stem
of an American Indian Peace Pipe

countries where hollow rattans and bamboos abound. And a more gruesome example, which is attributed to the savage hill tribes of Southern China, was made in a similar way from the thigh bone of a child.

But it is not only primitive tribes who have made use of natural objects. The segment of a huge crab's claw, after the flesh had been removed, was pierced at the narrow end and smoked by a Cornish fisherman of Falmouth; and there are records which show that, as early as the seventeenth century, the Indians of Nova Scotia made similar use of lobster claws. Equally primitive, perhaps, is the English countryman's pipe which, once upon a time, was made from the natural elbow of tough gorse root.

' Earth-smoking ' is one of the oldest practices. A small pit was dug in suitable soil and a stick driven through the earth almost horizontally until the point reached the ' bowl '. The stick, when withdrawn, left a hollow tube which served as a stem, but the smoker had to lie flat on the ground in an exceedingly uncomfortable position. Such pipes can of course be made on some natural terrace, as they were by Indian soldiers in the trenches during the First World War, and it is then possible for the smoker to re-main upright. ' Earth-smoking ' was known amongst the Indians, in the scrublands of the Kalahari and in the grass and salt steppes of West and Central Asia. These areas and parts of South Africa have produced examples of portable ' earth-pipes ' which are formed from lumps of unbaked clay with an orifice in the side. It has been argued that such pipes lingered on in Africa after the development of later types because they afforded a means of surreptitious hemp-smoking – a dangerous and often a forbidden practice. Indeed, 'earth-pipes.' as a *genre* are a very early stage in the evolution of the pipe and are probably derived from the earliest known form of smoking – the drawing in of hemp smoke over an open fire (and later through a tube) which, as Herodotus reported, was the practice of Scythian tribes. The addition of an orifice or tube at the side of the fire (which is, in fact, the ' earth-pipe ') is but a small step. And it is now to the tube itself – another primitive, makeshift form of pipe – that some attention must be given.

In the West Indies and Central America, at the time of their discovery, pipes were not known, or, more probably, their use had been forgotten. Tobacco was taken either as a cigar or as snuff. A chronicler with Columbus in 1492 reported that the Indians of Hispaniola had always ' a fire-brand in their hand, and certain herbs for smoking '. The tobacco was in fact rolled in a maize leaf and it was a natural transition for some form of tube to be brought into use in order to achieve cooler smoking. Moreover, there is first century evidence to suggest that the Mayas of Central America, who gave rise to many Aztec and Mexican smoking customs which were later observed by the Spaniards, had known about tube pipes. In fact the stone carvings of their priests, who used to blow smoke over their peoples as a religious ritual, depict the use of a simple tube tapering towards the mouth. Thus, although it seems that the first pipe will never be dated, there is little doubt that the Mayas passed on their pipes to the Aztecs of Mexico, who are reported to have had tubes of tortoiseshell, silver and wood, and, long before Columbus observed Indian smoking habits,

many primitive tube pipes of wood, reed, bone and pottery
had been in use.

In Chapter I attention has already been drawn to the
Spanish historian Fernandez de Oviedo who, in a history
published in 1526, described the use in the Indies of a two-
pronged or ' Y ' shaped tube; this, as he points out, was
used for the inhalation of smoke from an open fire through
the nostrils. It is possible that Raleigh had seen tubular
pipes in use amongst the French Huguenots, the earliest explorers and colonists in Florida, where a cane pipe with an
earth cup had been seen during Hawkins' expedition about
1564. Such straight tubes, however, had the obvious dis-
advantage that they allowed the tobacco to fall out, and it
is possible that some distortion in firing tube pipes in pottery gradually developed the more convenient ' bent ' pattern. From 1573 there are written reports to show the increasing popularity of pipes with small bowls which the
explorers and sailors returning from America had introduced into England.

¶ *Early Indian Pipes*
It must not be thought, however, that all the earliest pipes
of North America were crude, makeshift tubes. For
example, the Indians of the great Algonquin race, which
included some of the famous tribes, were accustomed to
build over the graves of their dead earth-mounds that resemble the tumuli of English chalk-hills. Excavations in the
famous Mound City of Ohio have revealed many carved
and ornamental pipes of elaborate design which are the
forerunners of later European shapes. And the religious

observances of the Algonquins included totem worship, so that many of these pipes have carved upon them the animal which the tribes regarded as sacred. The characteristic shape has a bowl mounted on a riband-like base which is curved slightly downwards and projects equally in either direction.* Some of these closely resemble the tubes which, in medical and religious rituals – the two being almost inseparable in the minds of primitive people – were used for drawing out disease from the bodies of the sick. The Algonquin pipes were probably used for the same purpose, since it is known that tobacco held for them a sacred character and played an important part in such rituals.

Some of these pipes are mounted with carvings of owls, beavers, pigeons and herons, which are executed with a skill exceeding that of the Indians in similar work since the discovery of America. In some cases the bowl is made inside the carved animal; in others, a human head, reminiscent of fine examples of Egyptian sculpture, takes the place of a totem figure. The pipes taken from mounds of the Muskogee, who inhabited the South East of the United States, are of patterns evolved from bent-up tube pipes. And it was from the Indians of this region that most European countries learnt the practice of pipe-smoking.

The most interesting of all Indian pipes, however, are those which were used in the council circle when the question of peace or war was being debated, for, as described in Chapter I, the ascent and disappearance of smoke into the air was charged with supernatural power and mystery for the Indians. The pipes which were passed with sacred cere-

* See page 54

Two Papuan Pipes
(*British Museum Copyright*)

(*facing page 58*)

A Slate Pipe
of North West
American Indians

mony around the circle of Chiefs to ratify their decisions were long-stemmed and plain; those smoked at the declaration of war were equally plain, corresponding roughly to the Churchwarden with a large bowl, but the peace-pipes, peculiar to each tribe, had a marble bowl, an ash stem about 40 inches long and were elaborately decorated with horse-hair and feathers of various birds – each part of the decoration signifying some token of success in hunting or war.[1] By recognising the decorations of these Calumets or Peace Pipes many explorers among the Indians found their way; their safe passage and perhaps their lives depended on whether or not the Chief decided to put the Calumet to his lips. Some of the bowls were slightly decorated, and these simple, hunting Indians of the plains even made pipes from tomahawks. It is the significance of the pipes, however, which is the principal point of interest. Their workmanship does not compare with the carving in wood and slate for which the fishing tribes of the North West coast became famous. These peoples, renowned for their totem poles, were alone in their ability to carve in low relief instead of in the round, which was the practice of those tribes mentioned above who left their pipes in mounds to the East of the Rockies.

Before leaving the question of pipes in this continent, even a brief outline of the subject must draw attention to the examples found in the Arctic regions and the ice deserts of the North. Although the Eskimo has produced some interesting pipes in both wood and stone,[2] his most precious possessions are naturally made from his finest material – walrus ivory. The decorations on the thick stems of some

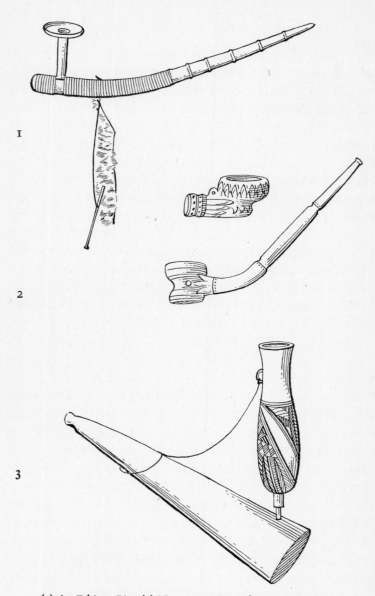

(1) An Eskimo Pipe (2) Nyoungwe Pipes from East Burma
(3) An African Dakka Pipe with a Wooden Stem

pipes from this material have made collectors regard them as their most valued specimens. In minute detail these real-istic sketches depict seal hunts, sledging expeditions, vil-lage scenes and innumerable Arctic animals. Many pipes of the far North, however, show European influence because, contrary to what might be expected, the Eskimo did not learn the craft of pipe-making from the Indians of the plains to the South. It was European traders who, having acquired it from the Indians, spread it across Europe and Asia until, in the sixteenth century, it reached China; and it was from the Chinese, by various intermediate stages, that the Western Eskimo learnt the craft. Thus, although the Eskimo's home lay in the continent that had given tobacco to the world, smoking had encircled the globe before it reached him. He, in turn, passed it on to hitherto non-smoking tribes of the Yukon district.

¶ *Some Eastern Pipes*

It is surprising that Europeans had anything new to teach the old cultured races of China and Japan. Yet most historians are impressed by the fact that tobacco and tobacco smoking were new things which appeared almost simultaneously in China, Japan and Persia at the close of the sixteenth century when the Portuguese were in power in the Indian seas. These Portuguese sailors, familiar with the West Indies, smoked cigars as a rule, and this form of smoking is now followed in parts of tropical Asia, such as Java and Burma; but the Portuguese were also familiar with the pipe of Brazil, and it may be that a simple Brazilian shape, such as a hollow nut with a straight reed or cane stem, was the prototype for all Far Eastern pipes.

Since the Chinese policy of exclusiveness, which Japan also adopted during the seventeenth century, kept intercourse with Europeans within narrow limits, it was natural for these countries to add to their pipes their own characteristics. The practice of mixing opium with the tobacco, which spread in China during the eighteenth century, developed a pipe with a small bowl like an acorn; it is usually made of metal and has a straight cane stem set at right angles. Though the Japanese pipe is smaller and daintier than the Chinese, the pipes of both countries are beautifully chased and ornamented with ivory, jade and lacquer. This miniature type of bowl passed into the interior of Asia and Siberia, and where, owing to the climate bamboo or cane is not available, the stem is often made of metal. Such pipes are smoked by the Tungus, by the Buryats of Mongolia and by the Tibetans.

Outside the influence of the Chinese pipe are the pottery bowls of the Shan States in Eastern Burma;* these bowls, ornamented with conventional representations of a bird, are used as touch-stones for testing gold and are very much more ornate than the crude wooden pipes of the hill tribes of the North and East of Assam. The latter, which have a conical bowl with the rim slightly higher in front than at the back, are also more likely to owe their origin to the Portuguese traders than to the Chinese pipes with small bowls.

The jungle tribes of the Malay peninsula, however, prefer

* See Nyoungwe pipes page 60

the cigarette and use a palm or banana leaf in which to roll the tobacco. But an unusual pipe, originating in Borneo, has passed to the Papuans in New Guinea. The stem is a section of thick bamboo with a tall, slender hard wood bowl. The practice among the Papuans, which appears to have spread to the Australian aborigines by the nineteenth century, is for one person to fill the large stem with smoke and then, having removed the bowl and closed the open end of the tube with his hand, to pass the pipe to each member of the company who inhales the smoke through his nostrils. When the stem is empty of smoke, the bowl is replaced and the ritual begins again.★

Primitive Malayan hill people in parts of the Philippine Islands still make straight tube pipes and pipes with bowls in wood, coloured pottery and brass, and it is interesting to note that the patterns they use are those learnt from the Spaniards in the seventeenth century. Their metal pipes, however, do not compare with the huge brass pipes of Sumatra which are in a class of their own. In fact the pipes in many Polynesian islands are quite distinct, for the use of tobacco did not spread to them from Malaysia. It was left to Captain Cook and his successors to teach the peoples of the Pacific, including the New Zealanders, the pleasures of smoking.

§ *Water Pipes*
The custom of cooling and cleansing the smoke of a tobacco pipe by drawing it through a vessel of water is one that was never found in America, nor has it been very pop-

★ *See plate facing page 58*

ular among Europeans; yet it was almost universal in the East and was practised also in Africa where the dakka pipe is found. All this strengthens the case for the fact that smoking had a separate origin in the Old World before the discovery of the New. The inhalation of hemp smoke in Africa undoubtedly dates from early times, but little is known about the transition from the tube pipes used for this purpose to the water-cooled dakka (so-called from the native word for hemp).* The insertion of a tube, which was filled with tobacco and which fitted into a horn filled with water, was probably the first method of cooling and mitigating the intoxicating effects of hemp smoke. The use of a horn was not ideal, and tribes around the Zambesi, who used the gourd and bamboo water-vessels, probably introduced one or other of these into the construction of the water pipe. The timberless regions of the Kalahari have produced examples of water pipes with stone bowls, while those from Nyasaland, for example, have wooden bowls that are carved with various geometrical designs.

When the Dutch founded Cape Town in 1652 they found dakka-smoking in full-swing. Tobacco then became popular and was often mixed with the hemp. Thus Kolben in his History of the Hottentots (1704) observed; 'Dacha is a thing of which they are likewise mighty fond. It banishes care and anxiety, say they, like Wine or Brandy, and inspires them with a million of delightful fancies.' He also described how women inured small children to the fumes of hemp or tobacco so that the smoking habit would be early acquired. This use of the dakka pipe, well known by

* See page 60

64

the Arab slave-traders, may have already been exported by them to Persia and India. A coconut, as a commonly used water-vessel in East Africa, had been substituted for the horn or gourd, and a long straight stem was found more convenient. This is a primitive form of the Indian Nargileh (meaning coconut), which was seen in India by an English visitor as early as 1615.[1]

The change in India from simple to more elaborate pipes may be traced in eighteenth century pictures in the British Museum. In one a lady can be seen smoking a more graceful type of Nargileh while being washed by her maids, and in another she is still holding the mouthpiece in her hand as, with her lover's arm around her, she gazes at a star-lit sky. Such pipes were equally popular among men and women in Persia in the seventeenth century. The idle women of the harems took tobacco all day long, and the use of the water pipe, cooling and cleansing the smoke as it did, went far to make this possible without ill effects. The Chinese also accepted the principle of the water pipe since it was well adapted to an opium and tobacco mixture, but, characteristically, they transformed the elaborate hookah into a neat portable pipe that can be held in the hand, with an upright stem curving towards the mouth. Such pipes are beautifully chased and inlaid with enamel.[2]

In Africa, in more recent times, the dakka pipe, popular from the Zambesi to the Congo basin, has been developed alongside the Nargileh which was reintroduced by the Arabs. It is therefore difficult to tell from which of these have been developed the many types of African water pipe.

[1] *See plate facing page 66*   [2] *See plate facing page 67*

¶ *The Myriad Pipes of Africa*

Although it is legitimate to suppose that hemp-smoking and the dakka pipe were indigenous to Africa, tobacco was almost certainly introduced by Europeans, and its popularity certainly spread into the most remote corners of the continent far in advance of the European trader and explorer. Thus the pipes of this continent show a remarkable variety and originality.

Seventeenth century accounts by early explorers describe the Negro's passion for tobacco and the use of huge pipes with reed stems, measuring six feet, and stone or earthen bowls, which held two or three handfuls of tobacco and rested on the ground; these were smoked by both men and women. But a straight tube pipe of bone has been found in almost universal use among the Berbers of North Africa, while a European type of pipe, showing Moorish influence in its decoration, is smoked by the richer members of the same area. Hence it is possible that the age old practice of inhaling hemp smoke through a tube persisted in the Sahara regions, as well as in South Africa, long after the arrival of the more sophisticated European pipe.

Broadly speaking, the huge forest regions, which stretch from the Gulf of Guinea through the Congo Basin to the Great Lakes, have produced elaborate wooden pipes, and the hot dry grassy Savannahs that lie to the North, East and South of these forests have produced pottery bowls which vary from crude makeshift pipes to beautifully finished specimens.

The natural curve of the primitive stem, which was made by rolling a leaf, is preserved in many of the later

An Indian Nargileh Water Pipe
(*Pitt Rivers Museum Copyright*)

(*facing page 66*)

A Chinese Water Pipe decorated with shagreen

(*facing page 67*)

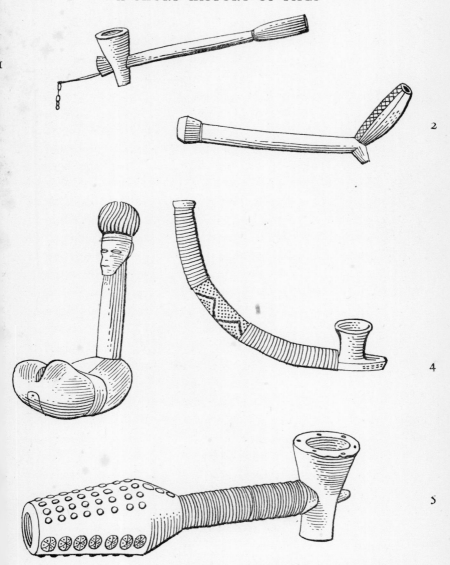

Pipes from West Africa: (1) Kasai River (2 and 3) Upper Ubanghi and
Welle Rivers (4) Ubanghi River District (5) Basoko

pipes of the Congo area.* The Monbuttu tribes, for example, made an elaborate wood and metal pipe with this remarkable curved stem which is sometimes bound with a ribbon of copper – an ostentatious display of wealth, for copper among these people ranks as gold among Europeans. Some of the pipes of this region, with an even more pronounced bow-shaped curve in the stem, are thick enough to hold water, and may carry tribal markings on the bowl. Ngombe has produced such a shape with a basket-work stem which is filled with red paste in order to make it air-tight, and the Manja people of the Upper Shari mount both stem and bowl in a heart-shaped fruit which is filled with grass and fibre to catch the tobacco juices and act as a filter. The drawings on page 67 suggest the variety of pipes in the Congo basin. More spectacular, perhaps, are those carved from wood by the Bali of the Cameroons, for these represent the huge and hideous fetishes or ancestral figures which are so common in West African utensils and ornaments. Although some of the pipes of the coastal districts are plainer and more European in design, the Ashanti make red pottery bowls which are picked out in white with various animals that at one time had significance as totems.

In the North of the Continent, the Sudanese, with the Mohammedan influence behind their higher type of culture, are not so concerned with fetishes. They have ' bent ' pipes with slender bowls and long stems so that the pipe hangs down from the lips like those of Holland. In Nigeria, where the work of the smith is favoured, they prefer iron pipes, although they also make some pottery bowls with

* See opposite

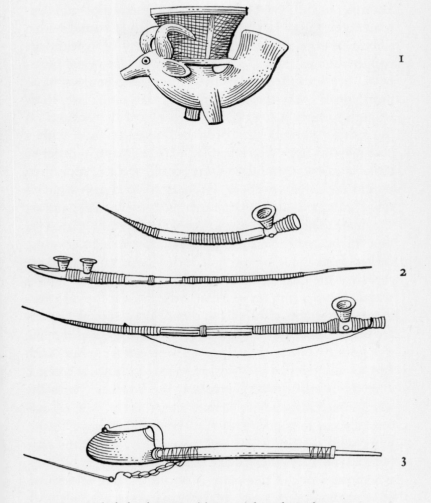

(1) A Mahsikulumbwe Pipe (2) Copper-bound Monbuttu Pipes
(3) A leather-bound Nigerian Pipe

leather jackets for protection. Indeed, to the south of Lake Chad, graceful pottery bowls abound, though suddenly, among the Nilotic peoples, the custom changes again and they, sitting on the ground, still pass from hand to hand a cumbersome pipe with a clay bowl which is fastened by hide to a long wooden stem and has a pomegranate-shaped gourd as a mouthpiece.

In Uganda and Tanganyika simple pipes are used, but from the west of Lake Nyasa come examples of heavy wooden pipes which are carved to imitate human bone. Many of the natives in these regions, however, prefer the use of snuff to these intimidating pipes which suggest, all too clearly perhaps, the way in which they were once made. Again, a little further west, in the upper Zambesi basin, there is an entirely different and unusual form of pipe with a shallow basin-shaped bowl in black pottery which is supported by the figure of an animal – antelope, buffalo or hippopotamus – and has a long stem that allows the bowl to rest on the ground.★ These are more interesting than most of the pipes of the Cape where, since the seventeenth century, the Hottentots and later the Kaffirs have copied the shapes of Dutch clays; some of them, however, are finely worked with inlaid wood, or serpentine – the soft greenish rock which is mottled like a serpent's skin and takes a high polish. It is more interesting, perhaps, to glance towards the Mediterranean shores to see what difference the modern material, briar, has had upon the pipes of Africa. Here, among the elaborate Moorish designs in Algerian briar, set with precious stones, can be found the pipe of the poor

★ *See previous page*

70

Clay Pipes

Arab – a man who yearns for tobacco as much as anyone. His meagre pipe, which is often made from a hollowed-out nut with a reed for a stem, sends a pitiful whisper across the Atlantic to Brazil, whence it came hundreds of years ago.

¶ Clay Pipes

The earliest Elizabethan fairy or elfin pipes have a barrel-shaped bowl leaning forwards, which has a flat ' heel ' and a twelve inch stem. Such clay pipes, it is believed, were made at Broseley in Shropshire as early as 1575 when pipe-smoking in England was in its infancy. By the beginning of the 18th Century, when a spur on the base of the bowl took the place of the flat ' heel ' (so that makers began to put their initials on the side of the bowl,) it was Broseley that supplied many of the new ' fancy ' clays with bowl mouldings in relief. To suit the more leisured life in London Coffee Houses and Clubs, the first Churchwardens and long-stemmed London Straws, with spurs which prevented the hot bowl from touching the table, began to make their appearance. On account of the popularity and perishable nature of clays, the industry began to thrive and pipe-makers set to work in various parts of the country. Although the comparison of prices with those of to-day is particularly misleading, clays were cheap: in the reign of Queen Anne, three dozen of the ' best ' English pipes cost eleven pence, and a gross of Dutch clays (which were in serious competition) cost two shillings.

The modern collector is mainly interested in dating clay pipes and, by size, shape and makers' mark, deciding on the workshop from which they came. A good collection should

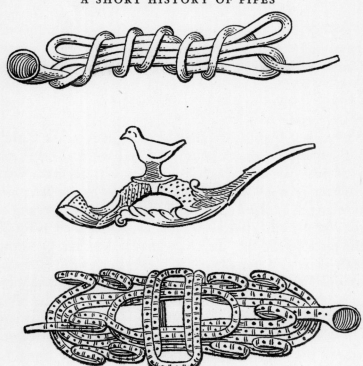

Staffordshire-ware Pipes

also show the ember tongs for lighting them before the days of matches, and the iron holders in which they were cleansed by the fire. A few clays are still made in England, and this ancient craft is discussed in Chapter V.

¶ *Some European Pipes*
As we have seen, pottery and porcelain manufacturers have often made use of the pipe as an example of their craft. Though the value of such work may be aesthetic rather

73

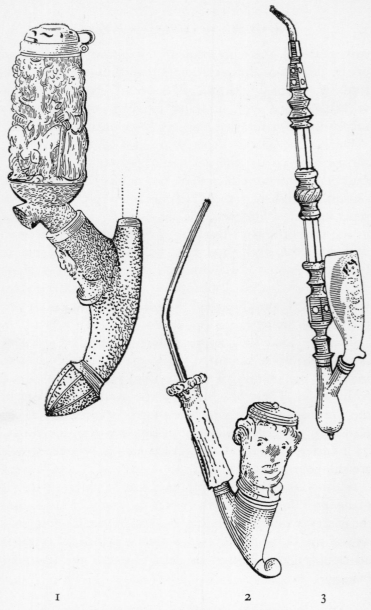

European Pipes: (1) Bavarian (wood) (2) Tyrolese (horn)
(3) German (porcelain)

than practical, there are probably no more colourful and ornate designs in European pipes than those made in Staffordshire pottery,* Bristol glass or, to give an example which also has fine smoking qualities, the elaborately carved meerschaum that has been so popular in Germany.

During the Thirty Years War, 1618-48, when soldiers carried tobacco and the practice of pipe-smoking all over Europe, it was the Dutch clay, not unlike the seventeenth century English pattern, which became the prototype for pipes in central Europe. This old shape is closely reflected in the proportions of the long, porcelain decorated bowl with its ' lean over ' and spur which was so popular in Germany, Austria and Switzerland. In the later types, however, the bowl is usually mounted parallel to a long stem with a curved mouthpiece so that all tobacco juices run into the base of the pipe.

There is something appropriately austere in the heavy bowls that are so common in Russia and which, like so many of the utensils of the Slavonic peasant, are carved from wood. These bowls follow the stout proportions of the Turkish chiboque which was introduced into southern Russia by the Turkish Army in the seventeenth century. Its influence has spread and similar carved wooden bowls are still common in Finland.

If the Corn-Cob pipe of the United States (which is made from the hard stem that bears the grains of maize) and the cherry-wood pipes of England and France have, mainly on account of their cheapness, a certain popularity, there is no doubt that no other modern pipe has the smoking

* See page 73

qualities and durability of the Briar. Ephemeral fashions must continue as long as smokers can be encouraged to try something different, but the great majority of pipes smoked throughout the world to-day, sometimes in shapes which re-echo the early primitive designs described in this chapter, are made from briar root.

We may well guess what pipes we might have to-day were it not for the French pipe manufacturer who, on a visit to Napoleon's birth place, is alleged to have broken his meerschaum and to have ordered a Corsican peasant to copy it in the local briar. Doubtless someone else would have discovered this valuable material. As it was, the first specimens of briar were sent to St. Claude – a remote village high in the Jura mountains, where the villagers, following the example of the monks, had established a thriving wood-carving industry. From that day they turned their attention from work in the local box-wood to the manufacture of 'la pipe'. And so it is that the twentieth-century connoisseur surveying the pipes of many ages, the decorated and the simple, the ornate and the grotesque, selects his own pipe of self-seasoned briar for the excellence of its workmanship, the correctness of its proportions and, above all, for the beauty of its flawless, finely-grained bowl.

CHAPTER V

HOW PIPES ARE MADE

' Happy mortal! he who knows
Pleasure which a Pipe bestows . . .'

ISAAC HAWKINS BROWNE

Since this is a century in which Briar Pipes are the most popular and the most commonly made, the greater part of this chapter is concerned with their manufacture. Much careful preparation is given to the wood, however, before it reaches the pipe manufacturer, and it is therefore necessary to consider the interesting and arduous work in various countries around the Mediterranean where the rare and precious briar root is collected. But, first, it is important to clear up a common misunderstanding about the word itself.

¶ *Briar Root*

Brier or Briar are nineteenth century variants from the form ' bruyer ' – an English word which copied the French ' bruyère ' in referring to the White Heath (Erica arborea) or that species of heather from which pipes are made. ' Bruyer ' was erroneously identified with the old English word ' brere ', which meant originally any prickly, thorny bush or collection of bushes, and now usually means a wild rose bush. It must be understood, therefore, that the briar with which pipes are concerned is in no way connected with rose-briar.

The briar generally used for pipe manufacture is found principally in Mediterranean districts (Greece, Algeria, Southern Italy, Corsica, Sardinia and Sicily). In these regions a hot, intensely dry summer follows a mild and showery winter, and it is in the effort to pass successfully through the season of drought that the heath-tree has developed the huge close-grained, deeply penetrating roots that give it its special value. The quality of the soil, too, is important, and some of the best roots are those which have thrust their way into the rocky hill-side. But the heath is of very slow growth and, as will be seen, the amount of unsatisfactory briar which has to be rejected at every stage of its preparation is immense. It will therefore be understood that the difficulties of finding, unearthing and maintaining an adequate supply of good briar form a fundamental problem for all pipe manufacturers.

Good root is both rare and inaccessible. The large heath shrubs take so long to mature that the most suitable root may be 60 – 100 years old; indeed, some of the finest specimens may have been growing for 250 years. They may stand, as they do in the former Royal Forests of Rome, where dense undergrowth and scrub limit the use of road transport. In the rocky woodlands of Sardinia, for example, where the drier ground tends to make the root harder and where the country is less dense, the transportation of briar in pannier baskets, carried by hand or by mules over rough mountain tracks, is a slow and laborious task. Moreover, in all these Mediterranean districts, forest fires may cause extensive damage to the briar; in addition to the heath-shrubs which are destroyed – and large areas may be made value-

(*above*) An unusually large Heath Tree of great age (*below*) A Briar Root
(*facing page 78*)

less for fifty years—the sparks that fall on the exposed crust of the root make a point of entry for insects. The root, however, continues to grow and the small cavities made by sparks and enlarged by the insects are often not apparent until the wood is cut.

In most of the countries, the manufacturer, whose business it is to find, carry, cut and prepare the wood for shipment, normally buys by auction from the owner of the forest or the Government the right to draw briar at a certain sum per 100 kilos. for a period of years. He employs diggers, equipped with simple tools, who are prepared not only to cut the wood, but to fell trees, to build crude bridges and clear rough tracks – in short, to deal with the attendant problems of such work in difficult terrain. These diggers are often small-holders who are glad to earn extra money by this seasonal work. Singly or in groups they set out, but since the boundaries of each area are often only roughly defined, their competitive efforts often lead to trespass and to endless disputes between the owners of the adjoining areas.

When the individual digger has selected and unearthed the root, it may have to be dissected; the cracked and rotten portions have to be chopped out so that, from a massive root, one or two pieces of rough crust of the briar weighing about 10 lbs. may be all that the digger can put into his baskets. When he has a load, it is taken to the collecting point which may be a considerable distance from the part of the forest in which he is working. Here the pieces of root are stacked and covered with earth to keep them moist. In due course the foreman, who comes round to the collecting

Cutting Ebauchon

points with a lorry, examines the wood and pays the individual digger according to the weight of good briar he has collected.

From these collecting points the rough pieces of root are taken to a specially equipped saw-mill where they are stacked under heather and sprayed with water. In these primitive mills, skilled workers, sitting before circular saws, cut every piece so that it can be examined for cracks and flaws; they decide how to cut the wood into the 'ébauchon' – a roughly shaped piece from which a pipe may eventually be made. The speed and danger of such work demands its price from time to time, and in these simple mills around the Mediterranean coast some operators with mutilated hands are still at work. Moreover, the wastage of briar during this initial process of cutting and constant examination is considerable, for much of the apparently good wood, when opened up and examined, is found to contain flaws which make it valueless.

When the ' ébauchons' have been cut, examined and divided into four grades, they are boiled in water for twelve hours in order to kill any remaining life in the wood; then they are stacked in well ventilated drying sheds where the seasoning of the wood may take about six months. During this time the effects of drying will cause some of the 'ébauchons ' to split so that, when the wood is fully seasoned, they are again examined for defects. Since satisfactory

Grading Ebauchon

'ébauchon' must show good grain and be flawless, some of them are rejected altogether. Indeed, the wastage in the total preparation is so great that sixty heath-shrubs may be required to yield the wood for one perfect pipe.

The 'ébauchon' which passes these rigorous examinations is then, some six to twelve months after the root was first lifted from the ground, put into sacks and shipped in various grades from these Mediterranean countries to pipe manufacturers all over the world. The best grades are sent to London which has long been recognised as the home of first class pipes.

¶ *The Making of Briar Pipes*
There is no limit to the care which is spent upon a pipe of first quality. In the finished product the difference between the good and mediocre pipe is not always evident to the untrained eye: as with furniture, beguiling processes can lend a deceptive lustre to an indifferent article. Experience has shown, however, that the first-class pipe, which is demanded by the connoisseur for its appearance and lasting smoking qualities, requires some seventy to eighty separate processes in its manufacture.

The seasoning of the briar before it is sent to the manufacturer has already been described; but in days when supplies of good root are diminishing and when tenders do not always tally with the goods supplied, it would be surprising if all the 'ébauchons' reached the manufacturer in the required condition. In fact they are often damp and may require some days in a kiln at the factory before they are ready for cutting. Moreover, although the wood is graded and sent to the manufacturer in sacks which are suitably labelled, the blocks in a particular sack are seldom all the same size so that, after re-grading, one sack may yield the wood for pipes of many different shapes.

Briar pipes were originally turned by hand and uniformity of size was not of particular importance; hand-turning is in fact still used on pipes of special shape or when it may be necessary to take advantage of a particular grain. But since the demand for briar pipes increased and French manufacturers at St. Claude devised special machinery, most standard shapes have been produced by machines. This is the more necessary because a high proportion of 'ébauchons' show flaws when they are cut so that it is only by using the methods of a modern factory that sufficient good bowls can be produced at a reasonable price.

In a modern bowl-turning factory it is probably the speed and dexterity of the operator of every machine which impresses the uninitiated spectator; it should not be forgotten, however, that in all the processes which are to be described, someone is responsible for the correct adjustment and accurate performance of the machines. A high degree of skill is required in grinding and setting cutting knives for every shape of pipe to be turned; in this work the machine has developed rather than effaced the original craftsmanship of the pipe-maker.

¶ Bowl Turning

If the first impression in such a factory is one of noise, the source of the loudest noise is an operator at a circular saw whose task is to trim the rough blocks to the size required

The Bowl Turning Machine

for the other machines. When this has been done, the block is passed to the Bowl Turning Machine (*Machine à ébaucher*). The operator places it in a chuck which is either closed by hand or by the automatic effect of centrifugal force when the lathe head is set in motion. The block, which is spinning at high speed, is approached by a heavy slide on which are mounted four knives to perform the actions of roughing, shaping, boring and facing the bowl.

At the Stem Turning Machine (*Machine à varloper*) the movement of the block is hand-controlled through an ingenious combination of cams and stops so that it is brought into contact with the rapidly turning cutter. The whine of the revolving blades changes into a raucous scream as, in a moment, they bite deeply into the briar to form the round or oval stem of the pipe-to-be.

An operator with a third machine (*Machine à fraiser*) takes over at this stage. The rough bowl is gripped internally by an expanding mandrel, and its base is rotated against a milling cutter which is ground exactly to the shape of the bottom of the bowl. After this operation there remain two little 'wings' of wood which are removed either by another, similar type of machine or by hand-filing.

In the case of 'bent' pipes, in which the bowl meets the stem at an acute angle, some variation of this sequence is required because the bowl would get in the way of the cutters of the Stem Turning Machine. The stem is therefore turned on the first machine when it has been re-set; the

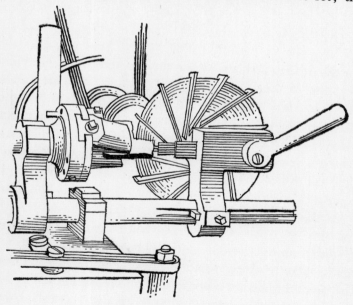

The Stem Turning Machine

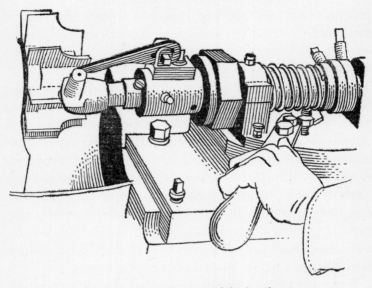

Shaping the bottom of the bowl

surplus wood is roughly removed on a saw before it is sent to the third machine, and the ' wings ' are removed by hand, either by filing or by holding the bowl against a special milling cutter. Great care is therefore necessary to preserve a perfect shape.

¶ *Stem-Drilling*

Care and accuracy are also required in this process because, if the bore is not central, the bowl is useless. The *Machine à percer*, which is designed for this operation, has a peg on a slide that holds the inverted bowl so that the operator can move it backwards and forwards on to a fast revolving drill. The drill is lubricated from time to time and the process continued until the bore just reaches the base of the bowl.

¶ Grading

The important task of grading the roughly finished bowls helps to explain the wide variation in price between two pipes which, to the layman, may appear almost identical. At this stage, bowls are usually classified as 'clean' or 'flawed' and both categories are sub-divided into three different grades which are clearly recognised by pipe-manufacturers. Each of these is suitable for the production of a particular class of pipe. Many of the bowls show such large holes after turning that they are useless and must be rejected; the majority have flaws of varying sizes and these, when they have been cleaned out, are filled with mastic or putty.

If the pipe-manufacturer does not make his own bowls, he buys a ' selection ' to suit the market he supplies; the amount of labour and the quality of the material he uses in finishing the pipe will, to some extent, determine the grades of bowl that he chooses. These finishing processes, which are described later, vary considerably from one manufacturer to another.

¶ Preliminary Polishing

After grading, the bowls are still not ready for the final processes. Further work by hand is required. The 'wings' of wood left on the stem by the third machine are removed on a coarse sand-paper wheel and the bowls are then completely sand-papered to remove any other surface irregularities. They are then polished on felt wheels with the aid of fine pumice powder mixed with oil. Such work helps to reveal the natural grain and so assists the next stage of selection.

In all these initial polishing processes the work is ' free-hand' and great skill is necessary, not only to achieve speed, but more importantly, to ensure that the shape of the bowl is meticulously observed. Too much pressure will spoil the shape; too little will not smooth the bowl sufficiently, and an uneven touch will leave diminutive bumps. It therefore takes at least two years to give a basic training to the polishers, who are frequently women, for one unnecessary touch of an abrasive wheel may mean that a good bowl is ruined.

The ' clean' bowls – alas, so few in number – are always examined after pumicing because they are selected mainly for their grain. The nature of briar root is such that perhaps only two or three bowls in every gross turned may be considered perfect specimens, although this figure will naturally vary with the quality of the ' ébauchon ' and the standard of the particular factory.

§ *Making The Pipe*
The final processes depend very much on the quality of the pipe in question. A manufacturer adapts his methods con-siderably to suit his market, so that a bowl of a lower grade does not have the same care lavished upon it as one of a higher quality.

Bowls with flaws of varying sizes undoubtedly form the majority of pipes sold to-day, and this does not mean that many of them do not give good and lasting service. The methods by which they are made vary little from one factory to another. After filling with mastic, the bowl is pumiced, and the stem is then machine-bored to take the vulcanite mouthpiece. These mouthpieces are 'moulded' (as distinct from the 'hand-cut' type which are fitted to more expensive pipes) and are stocked ready-made in the factory in a variety of shapes which only need to be trimmed to fit the stem of the bowl. When the bowl has been stained to the required colour and varnished to give it an attractive appearance, the whole pipe is polished on a mop. When, in the cheaper grades of pipes, a 'crusty' or gnarled appearance is required, the bowl is roughened on a suitable milling cutter before the finishing stages begin.

In a more elaborate and expensive process, requiring heavy and specialised equipment, the natural grain is preserved in pipes with a roughened appearance by subjecting the bowls at an early stage to the effects of heat and of high pressure sand jets. The soft wood is thus removed and the hard grain stands out in bold relief. After such treatment, the bowl is both light and tough.*

It has already been emphasised that in the case of the faultless pipe there is practically no limit to the care and patience given in every stage of its manufacture, and the final processes vary considerably from one factory to another. These are processes, closely guarded by each manufacturer, which aim at improving the smoking qualities and the lasting appearance of the briar and which make the good pipe an expensive article. Some thirty operations may be required and nearly all of them call for skilled craftsmanship.

* See plate facing page 90

The selected bowl undergoes further polishing both inside and outside on felt mops. It is then ready for various operations which are designed to develop its colour. Colour-finishing a pipe is considerably more difficult than that of other wooden articles on account of the natural hardness of the briar root and the various seasoning processes that the wood has undergone. Moreover, the manufacturer's aim is to make the most of the polish that can be obtained from the natural wood. At certain stages, however, stains may be introduced to accentuate the grain and further polishing takes place.

Various seasoning processes may be employed, some of which make use of nourishing oils, and are followed by a drying period which leaves the pipe bowl with a hard, permanent 'finish'. It is then ready for fitting with a first-class hand-cut mouthpiece. This is cut from solid sheets of vulcanite which is made to the most exacting specifications. The strip is bored, and the mouthpiece peg is turned by hand on a lathe. Next, the bowl is placed in a chuck and the bore is completed. The two parts can then be assembled. In this, precision is vital; the craftsman who performs the difficult task must gauge the amount the vulcanite will contract when it cools from the friction caused by his chisel so that the two parts fit each other perfectly. Finally the mouthpiece is tapered until a shape, appropriate for the bowl, emerges from the solid.

The next stages are concerned with shaping the fitted mouthpiece more accurately, and forming the ' button ' by which it is gripped in the teeth. Two further drilling operations have to be carried out to open the end (performed on

Pipes roughened by heat and sand

(*facing page 90*)

A fine example of a hand-carved Meerschaum Pipe of the
Nineteenth Century. Its texture and design suggest why
such pipes, popular in the ' Smoking Rooms ' of the Victorian era, had to give way to the Briar

(facing page 91)

a wide-boring machine) and to enlarge the smoke-hole.
The mouthpiece is then pumiced on a felt wheel to remove
the marks and scratches of files and abrasives.

Again, in the final stages of polishing the methods of
various factories differ, but the aim is to bring out the in-
herent beauty of the briar. After all this labour and care,
however, some blemish or fault that has become apparent
during the polishing may make it necessary, at the very last
stage, to reject the pipe as a failure. The expert who makes
this ultimate inspection considers the grain, the texture of
the briar and the workmanship: all must reach the standard
set by the prestige of the particular manufacturer.*

¶ *Clay Pipes*
Although the arrival of the briar pipe and the cigarette in
the Nineteenth Century crippled the clay-pipe industry,
' clays ' are still being made in England to this day. In addition to the short, cheap ' clay ', which is still to be seen in
the nursery and at the fair-ground, some demand continues
for Churchwardens with their 24 inch stems, ' Smoke
Room ' pipes and the thin-stemmed ' London Straws '.
This branch of the pottery industry is almost obsolete,
however, and although the craftsman's skill still lingers in
Shropshire, the clay which he handles is brought from
Devon. This, superior to the clay of Staffordshire or Dorset,
produces a fine, white ' finish '.

The dry clay is soaked in water and brought to an even,
plastic form by hand ' wedging ' or by being passed

* *Some further comments on the merits and defects of pipes in general will be found in*
Chapter IX.

through a ' pugmill '. When it has reached the right con-
sistency, it is rolled by hand into ' dummies ' of the lengths
that are required for the various sizes of pipe. After these
have set, each ' dummy ' is skilfully threaded with a steel
wire to form the air-hole, and is then placed in a mould to
give it the required shape. An iron stopper to form the
bowl is inserted, and the moulds, some of which have elaborate decorations, are put under pressure.

When the pipes have been partly dried, they are scraped
to remove any marks or rough edges, and the trade stamp is
impressed on the shank of each. An ornamental twist may
be put into the stems of ' Churchwardens ' so that the fingers of the smoker can hold them at the point of balance.

After the short pipes have been dried and the longer ones
moistened with water, they are put into ' saggars ' or earth-
enware firing pots and treated with China clay dust. These
' saggars ', shaped to curve the stems of the longer pipes,
are then piled up inside a kiln which may fire from 200 –
500 gross of pipes.

After the pipes have cooled, the tip of the stem is prepared with a spirit varnish, and a few are fitted with a
mouthpiece.

¶ *Meerschaum Pipes*
Special processes are required for pipes made from this
white mineral composed of magnesia, silica and water,
whose name literally means ' foam of the sea.' When
mined, it is soft and dry and forms a lather like soap. It
varies greatly in density, some lumps floating and others
sinking in water. That of medium density forms the best

1

2

3

Clay Pipe Making: (1) rolling dummies (2) threading the stem
(3) pipes in the saggar

pipe. Softness, lightness, purity and power of absorption are its main characteristics.

At the factory the blocks, which are shipped mainly from Asia Minor, are roughly shaped by circular and hand saws. They are rotated in a chuck in order to bore and to shape the bowl and stem. The whole is then smoothed with fine sand-paper. After polishing by hand with pumice and French chalk, the bowl is ready for immersion in various hot waxes, after which it receives a final polishing. It is the effect of the wax upon the meerschaum which later allows it to produce its characteristic deep rich colouring when it is heated by burning tobacco. Such pipes are usually fitted with amber mouthpieces.*

There are various imitations of meerschaum. Burnt gypsum slaked with lime or a solution of gum-arabic forms a hard plaster which, when smoothed and polished with oil, assumes a marble-like appearance. Another fair imitation of meerschaum is made from hardened plaster of Paris, polished and tinted with a solution of gamboge and dragon's blood, and afterwards treated with paraffin oil or stearic acid. There is no absolute test for meerschaum and even experts may be tricked by appearances. In absorption and colouring properties, the imitation is equal to the genuine article; but it is impossible to fake the lasting smoking properties for which genuine meerschaum is famous.

* See plate facing page 91

CHAPTER VI

CIGARS

' Sublime tobacco . . .
   Divine in hookas, glorious in a pipe,
   When tipp'd with amber, mellow, rich and ripe:
   Like other charmers, wooing the caress
   More dazzlingly when daring in full dress:
   Yet they true lovers more admire by far
   Thy naked beauties – Give me a cigar!

BYRON   *The Island*

¶ *The Rise and Decline of Cigar Smoking*

Explorers with Columbus found natives in the Cuban jungle smoking rolled up tobacco leaves in the form of crude cigars. In 1527, Bishop Bartolomé de las Casas, who went with the Spanish to America as a missionary, is quoted by Corti as having written: ' The herb which the Indians inhale is rolled up like a sort of bundle in a dried leaf . . . They then light one end of it and draw in the smoke at the other; the effect is a certain drowsiness of the whole body accompanied by a certain species of intoxication, in which state they declare that they no longer feel any sense of fatigue.' Since this habit became very popular amongst the Spanish sailors in the many ships that then plied between America and Spain, cigars soon reached Europe although they did not spread far beyond the frontiers of Spain and Portugal for many years. It was not in fact until the tobacco pipe had held its popularity for about

95

two centuries – and in England, at least, had lost it again because of the increasing fashion for snuff – that the 'Cigarros' of Spanish America and the 'Segars' of English America began to circulate widely in Europe.

By 1779 a German had secured from the Papal government the exclusive right for five years to manufacture cigars in Germany. Soon afterwards factories, modelled on Spanish principles, were set up in France and Hamburg, for the Napoleonic Wars had helped to encourage smoking throughout Europe and the smoking of cigars in particular. How the French and British Armies became acquainted with cigar smoking during the Peninsular War has already been discussed in Chapter I, and it is therefore only necessary to remind the reader of the vogue for cigars which steadily increased in England during the first half of the Nineteenth Century. Smoking-rooms were opened in fashionable clubs, and the snuff trade diminished rapidly on account of the return of smoking.

There is no evidence, however, that cigars were made in England before 1830. In that year a small business was started and it naturally prospered. Several cigar manufacturers exhibited in the Great Exhibition of 1851. These early British cigars were straight, and then, because a 'bellied' shape won popularity, wooden moulds were introduced into the manufacturing process. But no sooner had the cigar trade reached its height in the mid-Victorian era than the cigarette, which had won popularity among English and French troops in the Crimea, began to challenge the monopoly. This was something more than a novelty, and the reasons for its success have been discussed elsewhere in this book. It was cheaper for a man to roll his own cigarettes than to buy ready-made cigars, and the new demand soon brought about a response from the tobacco-trade. About 1860 British manufacturers began to make cigarettes with a better quality tobacco so that, as an immediate result, the cigar trade began to recede. Although there always has been and, it must be hoped, there always will be a demand for what can be the finest form of smoking, the mounting pressure of tobacco duties in Britain has had, and is having increasingly, the inevitable result. In the United States, Holland and Germany, however, cigars continue to be popular.

¶ The Home of Cigars

Although the demand for cigars and, to some extent, their manufacture has spread throughout the world, the islands of Cuba and Jamaica, where the crudely rolled leaves were first seen by Europeans, have remained the home of the best cigars to this day. This is largely due to the fact that the cigars are made in the same conditions of humidity in which the leaf is grown. Less good, but acceptable even to the connoisseur, is the cigar leaf grown in Java, Borneo and Sumatra in the East Indies, the United States, India, Japan and South Africa. And the cigars made in Britain (the price of which is lower than that of imported cigars because duty is paid only on the imported leaf) are also of excellent quality. Many are made from the same tobaccos as Jamaican cigars; a few are made entirely from Havana tobacco, such as the Vuelto Abajo leaf which comes from the best growing district in Cuba. The quality of such cigars is partly due to the British manufacturers' privilege of buying in almost any of the world's markets.

¶ *Growing, Curing and Grading the Leaf*

The many operations necessary in preparing tobacco for the factory have already been described in Chapter II, and there is little that need be added for the growing of cigar leaf in particular. Some of the plants that are transplanted from seed-beds into the open fields are protected from the full strength of the sun by screens of fine cloth; this produces the finest quality 'shade-grown' leaf which is often used for 'wrappers'. (Outside Cuba, some of the finest 'wrappers' are grown in the East Indies.) Then, after weeks of careful cultivation, which includes the fighting of pests and diseases and the 'topping' of each plant so that the leaves achieve maximum growth, the leaves are picked as they mature, tied on to laths and taken to the curing barns. After curing, the 'hands' are stacked in bulks to begin the long, natural process of fermentation.

Before marketing, the leaves are sorted for the purposes for which they are required. First, the small broken leaf is selected for the 'filler' or main body of the cigar. Secondly, the slightly imperfect leaf is taken as an inside wrapper for this 'filler'; this is called the 'binder'. Thirdly, the finely textured, probably 'shadegrown' leaf of first class appearance is selected as an outside 'wrapper'. For its journey to the manufacturer the leaf is packed under pressure in hogsheads in which the slow fermentation process continues. Several years may elapse before it is ready to be made into cigars.

¶ *The Manufacture of Cigars*

The 'wrapper' of a cigar may not come from the same country as the 'filler'. Many with a Jamaican filling, for example, may have a 'wrapper' from the Havana region of Cuba so that they are indistinguishable in appearance from the all-Havana cigar. Because leaf varies in quality, aroma and strength, the blending of different leaves is a vital stage in all tobacco manufacture.

The very best cigars are still made by hand and great skill is required to roll them in a uniform size. After the leaf has been moistened, the 'wrapper', 'binder' and 'filler' grades are all stemmed by hand or machine. Each 'wrapper' and 'binder' leaf is then smoothed out and put into a small stack which is folded over once and tied. In American factories the 'filler' is sometimes sprayed with a flavouring.

Cigars are rolled by hand on a flat board, and the only tools that are used are scissors to trim the leaf, a knife to cut the 'wrapper', and a cutter-gauge to trim the lighting end. The cut 'filler' is laid on the 'binder', which usually consists of two pieces of leaf of the appropriate size, and is rolled into a 'bunch' of the approximate length, thickness and shape for the particular type of cigar. The addition of the half leaf used as 'wrapper', which is carefully selected for its appearance, flavouring and burning qualities, begins at the lighting end and is arranged in spiral fashion so that the small veins of the 'wrapper' run lengthwise; veins that run across the cigar are a sign of poor workmanship. The 'wrapper' is tapered off at the head and retained by a tasteless gum.

In some factories the 'bunch' is formed in a block that contains about 20 moulds of the required shape and size.

H

When the lower half of the block has been filled with 'bunches', the upper half is placed in position and held under pressure for several hours. The 'wrapper' may then be applied by hand. For cheaper cigars, however, there are machines that open the block moulds, remove the 'bunches', cut and apply the 'wrapper' and finish off the cigar. Such machines turn out about 800 finished cigars per hour. Other machines are capable of preparing the 'binder' and 'wrapper' leaves and making the 'bunches'.

¶ *Colour, Size and Shape*

After selection and grading, some cigars are tied in bundles with a silk ribbon, but the majority are still packed in rows in wooden boxes, the best of which are of cedar wood. Twelve or thirteen cigars of precisely the same shade are kept for the top row. The colour of the leaf is classified by letters which are marked on the side or bottom of the box as follows:

Claro (C C C) – light: Colorado-Claro (C C) – medium: Colorado (C) – dark: Colorado-Maduro (C M) – very dark.

The well known names with which cigars are prefixed, such as Corona, describe the size and not the make. The following names indicate a gradual increase in size from $3\frac{1}{2}$ inches in the first to $7\frac{1}{2}$ inches in the last:

Half Corona: Très Petit Corona: Petit Corona: Corona: Corona Grandee: Lonsdale: Double Corona.

Some manufacturers give a special number to Cigars of a particular shape and size.

In addition to the standard round-headed cigar with parallel sides, there are other popular shapes. *Perfecto*, which has a pointed head and tapering sides, is particularly popular in the United States; *Panatella* is long with a rather small diameter and straight sides; *Cheroots*, a type that is characteristic of India and the East, are simplified cigars of various sizes and have open ends. *Whiffs*, though similar to *Cheroots*, are usually smaller and milder.

¶ *The Band*

The significance of this has often caused controversy. Early cigar manufacturers burnt their names and that of the brand on to the lids of their boxes; this practice, however, allowed the unscrupulous to make use of such boxes for the sale of inferior cigars. Individual cigars were therefore marked with a small label or star of coloured paper that was pasted on to each, but it was found that if these were burnt in smoking the taste of the cigar was spoilt, or if the label was torn off, the ' wrapper ' was often torn as well. This therefore led to the paper ring or ' band ' which, with care, can be removed easily without spoiling the cigar.

Markings and terminology have led to various disputes between manufacturers. Until the early years of this century even Continental and British cigars were often labelled ' Havana '. This practice became so harmful to the sale of the genuine product that, in 1907, the Cuban cigar was protected against cheaper imitations. Various courts have since held, however, that Spanish terms for colour, shape and size are not objectionable, but it remains an offence by British law to use the term Havana for cigars that have not been made there.*

*Some comments concerning the Selection, Smoking and Care of Cigars will be found in Chapter IX.

CHAPTER VII

SNUFF

'You abuse snuff! Perhaps it is the final cause of the human nose.'
                                                S. T. COLERIDGE

There is nothing new about the taking of tobacco in the form of snuff. American aborigines are known to have mixed finely ground tobacco with other plants such as yew, sumac and willow, to have flavoured the mixture with various barks, musks and gums, and to have used animal bones, gourds and pouches for the storage of their snuff. The early Portuguese explorers found that the natives of Brazil made use of a rosewood pestle and mortar for grinding their powder, and the monk, Romano Pane, who accompanied Columbus on his second expedition in 1493, noticed that the Indians snuffed up tobacco powder through a tube. Long ago these practices spread. The exquisitely hand-painted snuff bottles from China, boxes of Yak horn from Tibet, African gourds, and shells from the West Indies –all these suggest how innumerable countries have, for centuries, prized not only snuff but the vessel in which it is contained.

The word ' snuff ', in the sense in which it refers to the powdered form of tobacco, is derived from the Dutch who are probably responsible for introducing it to Europe a short time before it reached England in the middle of the seventeenth century. It should be remembered that tobacco at this time was still regarded by some as a remedial, and snuff was prescribed by physicians in order to stop bleeding and to clear the head. After the Restoration of Charles 2nd in 1660, when the Court made many French customs fashionable, the taking of snuff as a social convention was firmly established in England. As a practice that was considered to be very much more refined than that of smoking, it had come into vogue among circles that imitated the Court in the reign of William and Mary, and the very novelty of snuffing made an increasing appeal to the gallants who led the world of fashion during the reign of Queen Anne. The beau who carried a tortoiseshell comb to improve the appearance of his flowing wig in public seems to have been as fascinated by the paraphernalia necessary for snuffing as his Elizabethan predecessor was delighted by the pipe-smoking equipment that he carried so ostentatiously to the Playhouse.

It was the custom for every dandy to grate his own snuff and for this purpose he had to carry a remarkable collection of equipment. First, the roll or twist of hard tobacco known as a ' carotte ': then the wooden grater (somewhat similar to a kitchen nutmeg grater) with a trough at one end to catch the snuff: and finally the snuff-box, wonderfully jewelled and decorated, the display of which could enhance his gestures and attract attention to the rings on his immaculate fingers. The tools to be found in any good collection of snuff-boxes show that his equipment could be even more elaborate. There was a pin, probably of silver, for pricking the holes in the grater; a hammer for tapping it; a rake for separating the coarse and fine snuff, and a spoon for taking it from the box. There was even a hare's foot for wiping the surplus snuff from the upper lip.

There seem to have been no bounds to the extravagance of the social custom which was so characteristic of the early eighteenth century. When gallants were proud to carry a small quantity of snuff in the heads of their canes, which were perforated so that the aroma could be inhaled, it is perhaps not surprising that, in the great age of satire, they became popular subjects for the satirists. An obvious example may be taken from Pope's ' Rape of the Lock '.

> Sir Plume, of amber snuff box justly vain
> And the nice conduct of a clouded cane;
> With earnest eyes, and round, unthinking face,
> He first the snuff-box open'd then the case ...

Nor were snuff boxes used exclusively by men. In 1712, the *Spectator* complained of snuff-taking as an impertinent custom adopted by fine ladies, equally disgusting whether practised sedately or coquettishly. For some of these ladies toyed with a box merely to display their pretty hands, but the woman of fashion thought nothing of pulling out her box in the middle of a sermon and of freely offering her best ' Brazilian ' to her friends. Indeed she might even have asked the churchwarden to take a pinch as she dropped her money into the collecting-plate.

In *Snuff and Snuff-Boxes* (1951), Mr. H. McCausland quotes the somewhat satirical commentary by a German, Johann Cohausen, in 1720:

' ... All classes snuff, from the highest to the lowest. I have sometimes wondered to see how lords and lackeys, High Society and the mob, woodchoppers and handy men, broom squires and beadles, take out their snuff-boxes with an air, and dip into them. Both sexes snuff, for the fashion has spread to women: the ladies began it, and are now imitated by the washerwomen. People snuff so often that their noses are more like a dust-heap than a nose; so irrationally that they think the dust an ornament, although, since the world began, all rational men have thought a dirty face unhealthy; so recklessly that they lose the sense of smell and their bodily health.

'They snuff without need, at all times, in all places, without rest, as though their fate and fortune, their name and fame, their life and health, even their eternal salvation depended upon it.

'Do but notice what grimaces snuff-takers make, how their features are convulsed, how they dip into their snuff-boxes in measured rhythm, cock up their noses, compose their mouths, eyes and all their features to a pompous dignity, and as they perform the solemn rite of snuff-taking, they look as if they scorned the whole world, or were bent, on some enterprise of which they might say, like Bouflet, "I will make the whole world tremble!"''

The most notable female snuff-taker of this period, as Mr. H. V. Morton pointed out in 'The Ghosts of London', was Mrs. Margaret Thompson who died in 1776 and whose devotion to snuff is made clear in her will. She directed that the bottom of her coffin be filled with unwashed handkerchiefs and a sufficient quantity of the best Scotch snuff to cover her body. The six greatest snuff-takers in the parish were to act as bearers and, instead of black, they were to wear snuff-coloured beaver hats. Snuff was to be strewn before the funeral procession and carried in boxes by her pall bearers for their refreshment as they went along.

If such was its vogue, it is not surprising that the preparation of snuff became more and more elaborate during the eighteenth century. By 1728 there were already many kinds, but the three main grades were the granulated, the powdered and the bran – or coarse part which remained after the second grade had been sifted. Perhaps the best known type is still ' rappee ', from the French word ' râpé ' meaning rasped or grated. A snuff-seller in 1740 made a list of prices for some eighteen different kinds of 'rappee,' including English, best English, high flavoured, low, scented, composite, and so forth. Snuff was procurable in brown or black, plain or scented, and 'rappee' still is, in most cases, the foundation of what are termed 'fancy snuffs'. Black 'rappee' was made of plain Virginian tobacco. During the eighteenth century, however, the Spanish bran was particularly popular and was sold with an aromatic rose-scented vinegar of Spanish origin at about £3 sterling per pound. Macouba was a snuff strongly perfumed with attar of roses, and Masulipatam, with its rather strong Oriental flavour, has maintained a popularity to this day.

' Smoking has gone out,' said Dr. Johnson in 1773, and though not wholly true, this was certainly an accurate comment on fashionable society. Smoking in the eighteenth century, as we have seen, was only enjoyed by the less conventional and the humbler classes of society. It was popular among the dons and undergraduates at Oxford and Cambridge, and the famous portraits of the period, whether written or painted, make it clear that neither

Some Snuff Boxes
(*Victoria and Albert Museum. Crown Copyright*)

(*facing page 106*)

squire nor country parson were often to be seen without a
pipe. Nevertheless, the Augustan Age in England was pri-
marily an age of snuff. As Mr. McCausland points out: ' A
wooden effigy of a Highlander in the act of dipping into his
horn snuff-mull or raising a pinch to his nose was by far the
commonest of the signs indicating where snuff was sold; in
various forms Highlanders appeared outside the premises
of snuffmen all over England in the eighteenth century, and
in a few cases still remain in use.'

The increasing sale of tobacco in the early nineteenth
century has already been mentioned in Chapter I. By 1850
the popularity of smoking had again drawn level with that
of snuff-taking, and, after the Crimean War, the cigarette,
with all its appeal to laziness, was beginning to spread with
ever increasing success across the world. Moreover, the de-
corum of the Victorian Age had no place for the large
gaudily coloured handkerchief of the eighteenth century
on which a few snuff stains made little difference; the effect on the neat white linen handkerchiefs was, however,
another matter and another reason why snuff was banned
from the Victorian household. Yet some professional men
and a number whose work made smoking impossible remained faithful to snuff. For obvious reasons it still continued to find its way into pulpit, law court and sickroom,
and remained popular with carpenters, tailors and crafts-
men whose hands are seldom free to attend to pipe or
cigarette.

Since the cigarette has enjoyed increasing popularity
from the beginning of this century and now absorbs four-
fifths of the world's tobacco supplies, it is perhaps sur-

prising to find that the demand for snuff is increasing once again. A million pounds are consumed annually in the United Kingdom and considerably larger quantities in the United States. Moreover, snuff, which was originally monopolised by the more fashionable members of society, is to-day making a much wider appeal. Large manufacturing and mining districts in the United Kingdom, where working conditions prohibit smoking, have the bulk of the trade, and it is said by retailers that snuff is becoming increasingly popular amongst women. In addition, since the consumption of snuff increased during the Second World War when cigarettes were in short supply, there is no doubt that increasing prices of tobacco have made many people discover that an ounce of snuff can be made to last as long as three or four ounces of smoking tobacco. It is therefore possible that the cigarette, which originally put snuff out of favour, may once again have its supremacy challenged by the growing demand for snuff.

Of the best method for taking snuff there is, and always has been, considerable dispute. Some take it between the thumb and forefinger, others from the thumb nail or back of the hand; perhaps the most stylish method is to place the pinch in the little hollow formed on the side of the wrist at the base of the bent-back thumb. But for one who would press the question further, it is necessary to turn to the literature of the eighteenth century where the whole etiquette of snuff-taking is set forth in the greatest detail.

¶ *Snuff Boxes*
Many magnificent boxes have been handed down from

generation to generation through three centuries, and they still exchange hands to-day for large sums. Such boxes are usually of exquisite workmanship, ornamented with diamonds, or cameos of delicate design. There has been much fine craftsmanship in the work on boxes in gold and silver and many types of shell. Even the ordinary wooden kind, with such perfectly fitted hinges and lids, are notable for their workmanship. Some are very small but the majority measure four or five inches in length – a convenient size for the pocket of the spacious waistcoat of the past. Snuff, like claret, is thought by some to be improved if its chill is taken off, so that very thin boxes, decorated with red or fine gold, have been popular and are still to be seen in some collections. Some of the hand-painted decorations and miniatures on English boxes of glass, porcelain and papier-mâché are as perfect in their own way as the exquisite, internally painted snuff bottles from China.*

§ *The Manufacture of Snuff*

After the early days when snuffers made their own preparations, grocers and other tradesmen began to prepare it for them with a simple pestle and mortar. As the demand increased, British flour-mills in Scotland, Yorkshire, Derbyshire and the Lake District started to grind snuff; in fact three of these original water-mills are still working. Most factories to-day, however, make use of electricity, and, although a few 'mulls' are survivals from the eighteenth century, the majority of machines have been modernised. But the processes of manufacture have not undergone any fun-

* *See plate facing page 106*

damental change in two hundred years. Every factory is proud of its own secrets, especially those relating to the essences by which the snuff is scented, but the following sequence of events may be taken as standard procedure. Details will of course vary with the particular type of snuff, the manufacturer and the country in question.

Snuff may be either 'wet' or 'dry'. The first, which contains a higher moisture content and cannot therefore be inhaled so deeply, is still popular in Scotland. American manufacturers have a market for the so-called Copenhagen, Swedish and Polish snuffs which are used for 'dipping' or chewing – a practice that is still popular in Scandinavian countries also. In Britain, however, the largest sale is for 'dry' snuff, such as 'S.P.' which can be inhaled deeply through the nose and which, although sold in a variety of brands, has remained basically the same for two centuries. There is also a very large market for medicated snuff which, among other processes, is treated with camphor, menthol and eucalyptol.

¶ *Preparation of the Leaf*
When the leaf has been drawn from the bonded warehouse and the appropriate duty paid, it is taken to the factory where it undergoes the preliminary process of 'curing' and 'toasting'. This was not always the practice, however, for the superior quality of such snuff is said to have been discovered accidentally when a mill in Ireland caught fire and the burnt leaf became drenched with water. What was thought to have been destroyed was found to be superior in quality to the original unmoistened and untoasted leaf.

It thus became standard procedure to moisten the cut leaf and to spread it on trays so that it could be toasted in front of glowing coal. To-day machinery plays an important part in the drying of the leaf.

¶ Fermentation and Drying

For the best brands, such as ' S.P.' and ' S.M.', the whole of the leaf is cut and ground. The cheaper varieties, however, are made chiefly from the stem to which, after it has been finely ground, the flavouring is added.

In Britain, when the leaf has been cut, it is moistened and then allowed to ferment in a special conditioning chamber for about three weeks. The conditioned leaf is then dried in rotating gas-heated drums which have the effect of ' paning ' or slightly darkening it, as in the normal methods of tobacco manufacture. American manufacturers, producing a different type of snuff from dark air-cured or fire-cured tobacco, allow a fermentation period of four or five months and then allow the leaf to dry naturally. But manufacturers in Britain, who are prevented by high taxation from holding large stocks for long periods, are able to make smaller quantities of fine quality snuff in three or four weeks.

¶ Mulling

An automatic pestle and mortar, known as the Rough Mull or First Mortar, grinds the leaf into a coarse powder which is then ready for sieving. In a few factories the old type of mill-stone still performs this operation. Another method is that of pounding the tobacco to the required degree of firmness by a high speed Hammer Mill; or it may

Snuff Making: a large mortar

simply be ground again, after the Rough Mull, by a Large Mortar, shaped like a huge bucket, which may have as many as three rotating, heavily weighted and power driven pestles. Such a machine can grind about 80 lbs. of leaf in two or three hours. Both phases of grinding are covered by the term 'mulling' – a name which is also used for various brands of snuff.

¶ *Sieving*

Although the leaf emerges from ' mulling ' as a fine powder from which any particles of metal have already been
extracted by a magnetised drum, it is still not fine enough.
The powder is therefore fed on to automatically oscillated
sieves formed with cloth meshes that may have as many as
80 threads to the inch. During this process the powder may
be mixed with additional mulled leaf and the whole blend
resieved. From these fine meshes the powder gains its characteristic silky texture, and every vestige of foreign matter
which might act as an irritant in the finished product is thus
excluded.

¶ *The Essences*

The addition of the delicate and minutely adjusted aromas,
which make such fine shades of difference between innumerable brands of snuff, is, obviously enough, the key
stage in manufacture; the composition of these essences are
secrets which every manufacturer guards jealously. In
some factories the recipes have been handed down through
generations, and the exact ingredients may not even be
known by the employees who handle the snuff during this
stage.

After the snuff has been carefully examined for colour,
texture and general condition, the inorganic matter, such
as carbonate of potash, and the liquid essences are added.
They are then evenly distributed by a Mixing Machine.
In the finished product, Light snuff such as ' S.P.' carries
about 17% moisture, whereas a dark, ' wet' snuff has about
32%.

The commonest ingredients, whose scent may be used in the essences, include the genuine Chinese camphor flower, menthol (from crystals that may be mulled, or dissolved by spirit, and sieved), eucalyptus from Australia, the tonka bean from Venezuela, Brazil and Honduras, and Rose Otto from Turkey and Bulgaria. Innumerable ingredients may be included in the essence for a particular brand. Some that were popular in the eighteenth century, such as Bergamot, Lavender, Cassia, Lilac and Cinnamon, are still used; among many others, a few are as common as Orange and Lemon.

Every factory has its own method of adding the essences, but it may be done while the snuff is being agitated by the rotating wedges of the mixing machine. It is particularly difficult to get them evenly distributed, and a great deal of careful mixing is necessary. Moreover, snuff is at all times difficult to handle because it picks up extraneous smells very easily. Even two open tins on a shelf tend to exchange their respective scents, and many dealers and tobacconists have had a whole consignment ruined in this way.

¶ *Final Stages*

After mixing, the prepared snuff is allowed to lie in bins for several days because this maturing period helps to improve the texture and allows the strength of the aroma to develop. It is then weighed or measured into tins by simple methods which ensure that the snuff is not touched by hand.

The moisture content of all snuff which is prepared for export is tested by Excise authorities so that they can determine the exact amount of leaf which is leaving the country

Snuff Making: adding the essences

(*facing page* 114)

and ensure that the permissible amount of inorganic matter (25%) has not been exceeded. Snuff that is sold for use in Britain is tested from time to time by Excise authorities at the factory.

I

CHAPTER VIII

THE PRODUCTION OF FIRE

' Mr. Weller, senior, refilled his pipe from a tin box he carried in his pocket, and, lighting his fresh pipe from the ashes of the old one, commenced smoking at a great rate.'

DICKENS

¶ Primitive Methods

Although the Safety Match and the automatic Cigarette Lighter are modern, their evolution is part of the vast subject of fire-making which was man's earliest and perhaps his greatest achievement. The most primitive way of kindling a fire, as every schoolboy knows, was that of rubbing two sticks together, but the methods varied according to the type of wood available. ' Drilling ' – the method that was common among primitive peoples in America, Europe and Africa – involved the twirling by hand of a bluntly pointed stick in the shallow pit of a wooden hearth. In South East Asia the practice of ' sawing ' with a piece of bamboo was more prevalent, and in countries where corky wood is found, primitive tribes used to ' plough ' one stick up and down a groove in the grain of another. In each case the dust thus produced could, with care, be fanned into a glow which ignited the ' tinder '. This term refers to any highly inflammable substance which will nurture a spark until it can be fanned into an active blaze. Aboriginal tribes used grasses and plants; the old-fashioned tinder-box of

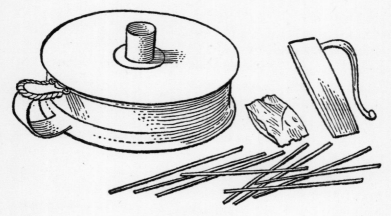

An English Tinder Box

more recent centuries used charred rags. The wood of a modern match is, in effect, 'tinder'.

Percussion was another ancient way of making fire which, after man had learnt to work iron, developed into the flint and steel method. After countless centuries this survives in the type of tinder box that was to be seen in every kitchen in England during the first decades of the last century. These boxes were usually round and had a socket in the lid for a candle. The steel, which was shaped to give protection against careless blows from the flint, was held in the left hand, and, depending on draughts and the condition of the 'tinder', it used to take from three minutes to half an hour to get a light. The 'tinder' was blown into a glow sufficiently hot to ignite the so-called match – a splinter of wood tipped with sulphur.

Similar boxes of superior metals – brass, copper, pewter,

Sheffield-plate and even gold – were used in living rooms of better class houses, and smaller boxes and pouches were carried in the pocket or affixed to the belt. These portable tinder-boxes were seldom used with sulphur matches, for smokers lit their pipes direct from the glowing tinder. In fact pipes, as often as not, were lit from a coal which was removed with tongs from the fire.

Some early tinder-boxes were made with a steel in the form of a wheel which projected at one side of the box. The wheel was rotated by means of a string wound round the axis pin, and the flint was held against its rotating edge. These, together with German types of the sixteenth century in which an iron flint-wheel was actuated by a coiled spring, were the forerunners of the modern lighter.

¶ *The Evolution of Matches*

At the time phosphorus was discovered accidentally in 1670, the word ' match ' (from the French ' mèche ' – a wick) simply referred to a prepared length of wick that would burn sufficiently steadily to fire a cannon or flintlock gun. The various types of 'Instantaneous Lights' which resulted from this discovery were still a long way from what is understood as a match to-day. Indeed, the risk of burns was such that the use of phosphorous for ignition lay dormant for about a century.

About 1800 ' Pocket Luminaries ' were introduced into London. These consisted of a bottle that was coated internally with phosphorus and some wooden matches that were tipped with sulphur; when the matches were withdrawn from the bottle, contact with the air produced a flame. Similar but more effective was the ' Instantaneous Light Box ' which had a stoppered bottle containing asbestos saturated with sulphuric acid; the matches in this case were tipped with chlorate of potash and sugar. Various matches prepared with phosphorus were tried out in the first decades of the 19th century, and in 1823 appeared the ' Dobereiner Lamp ' – a further attempt at what would now be termed a lighter. This ingenious device generated hydrogen gas so that it impinged upon a small quantity of platinum; through chemical action the platinum became incandescent and ignited the gas.

But there was nothing sufficiently reliable and practical to supersede the tinder-box until, about 1827, John Walker, a druggist of Stockton-on-Tees, introduced the Friction Match. This, the latest and best of all 'Instantaneous Lights', was made from a paste, not of phosphorus, but of chlorate of potash, sulphide of antimony, gum arabic and water: the head had to be nipped between the folds of a piece of sand-paper and withdrawn sharply. The price was one shilling per hundred. Similar matches called ' Lucifers ' followed shortly afterwards, and, in the 1830's, phosphoric friction-matches known as ' Congreves ' came into general use. But all early attempts at phosphoric matches were dangerous because, on occasions, they lit too readily, and the white phosphorus caused serious disease among the workers who made them.

Such matches were followed by ' Fuzees ', specially designed for lighting pipes and cigars, ' Vestas ', with a stem of long-burning wax-taper, ' Vesuvians ' and many others. By the middle of the century a harmless red form of phosphorus had been discovered and, in the form of Safety Matches, it was incorporated into the rubbing surface on the side of the box – not on the match-head. ' Strike Anywhere Matches ', using the dangerous yellow phosphorus that was later forbidden by law, continued to be made, and in 1898 a satisfactory substitute was found so that such matches could still be struck on any rough surface. To-day the ubiquitous domestic match, whether ' Vestas ' or ' Safety ', is as harmless as it is necessary.

Note: A detailed study of this subject lies beyond the scope of this book. The reader who wants to discover the precise difference between these and many other matches that have not been mentioned is referred to the displays in many museums, and to the books mentioned in the bibliography.

¶ *Lighters*

It has already been emphasised that there were various types of experimental lighters which threw sparks on to the tinder by means of a toothed wheel. Gradually a wick replaced the tinder, and the rare metal, cerium, was found to yield sparks more freely than the original ' flint '. In some Victorian lighters the sparks ignited (or failed to ignite) a small spirit lamp; others carried a piece of match-cord tinder in a tube affixed to the side. The latter were somewhat like the tinder-tube – a neat, pocket apparatus, with a separate flint and steel secured to the tube – which is still in use in France to this day.

During the 1914-1918 War, when it became important to find substitutes for matches, some friction lighters made use of a metal match containing a wick which was immersed in an inflammable fluid and struck in a serrated groove. With scrap materials, munition workers and soldiers imitated the crude types of petrol lighter which had been on sale for some years. These were by no means 'fool proof', but they all helped in the development of the first fully reliable lighters which appeared soon after the war ended.

In 1922, appeared the Dunhill lighter,* a pocket lighter which carried a substantial amount of fuel and which could be operated by one hand. Its reliability depended on the simplicity of its design and the care with which it was made, and it can be pointed out that, in lighters of various shapes and sizes, the design of this original model is still being used. Five years later Mr. Aronson produced a lighter which was operated by a thumb-piece that turned the flint wheel and extinguished the flame when the pressure was released. Both these lighters showed the importance of caps that fitted tightly over the wick in order to prevent evaporation. Both designs paved the way for countless shapes and sizes of lighter that have followed.

Now that the reliability of the petrol-lighter has been wholly proved, many experimental varieties have appeared in the last twenty years. There are lighters that make use of electricity; lighters with a catalytic action in which the fumes of alcohol, passing over a platinum element, cause it to glow or to ignite the vapour; an Everlasting Match, and lighters using gas as fuel have already gained some popularity. Meanwhile efforts have continued – somewhat un-

* See plate facing page 122

successfully, it seems – to perfect self-lighting cigars and cigarettes which, like a match, ignite when they are struck on the side of the packet. While experiments continue, the finest petrol and the finest gas lighters that money can buy still make use of the ancient principle of Flint and Steel. But, especially in an atomic age, who can say what the future may hold?

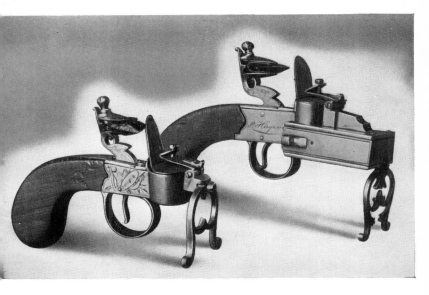

(*above*) The First Dunhill Lighter (*below*) Eighteenth Century Tinder Pistols

(*facing page 122*)

CHAPTER IX

THE PRACTICE OF SMOKING
'No woman should marry a teetotaller, or a man who does not smoke.'
R. L. STEVENSON *Virginibus Puerisque*

PIPES

Since so many men have affirmed that pipe-smoking is one of the most satisfying pleasures on earth, only inexperience and carelessness can account for those who, having a taste for smoking, have given up the pipe in despair. Many of these have undoubtedly been novices. Others are confirmed cigarette smokers who, at some time, have tried to smoke the wrong type of tobacco in an unsuitable pipe and, little caring how to fill or tend it, have expended a box of matches upon a single smoke and thrown away the offending pipe with disgust. Such experiences are sad but not uncommon. Indeed, many a confirmed pipe-smoker is too little aware that the difference between the good and the mediocre pipe is not always evident to the untrained eye. Perhaps it is only the connoisseur who does not need to be persuaded that so much depends on using a pipe that suits and pleases the individual smoker. Probably only he knows how to select such a pipe and, having selected it, how to look after it. He realises that the pipe is not quite so simple as it appears.

It is absurd to suggest that there is anything mysterious

or esoteric about the gentle pleasures of pipe-smoking. Yet, if full satisfaction is to be won, three factors have to be considered:

(a) The selection of a good pipe that is suited to the particular smoker.

(b) The maintenance, cleanliness and care of the pipe.

(c) The choice of a good quality tobacco of a suitable type.

(a) THE SELECTION OF PIPES

The reader who is interested in the rarer types of pipe, such as Meerschaum, Clays and Corn-Cob, will find information concerning them in Chapters IV and V. The average smoker, however, is more likely to be concerned with the selection of a Briar and this, the most popular type of pipe to-day, must therefore be considered in detail.

Experiments have shown that good briar is so tough and close grained that it does not readily absorb the ' tars ' contained in tobacco smoke and so become foul. As a general rule, the more wood there is in a pipe the more it absorbs heat and produces pure, cool smoke, but this requirement of coolness must also be matched with that of balance. The pipe must be comfortable in the mouth. Some smokers find their ideal in a heavy bowl while others, believing that the length of stem also helps to cool the smoke, prefer a smaller bowl with a longer stem. There are also some who think that the length of the stem should be provided largely by wood rather than by the vulcanite mouthpiece.

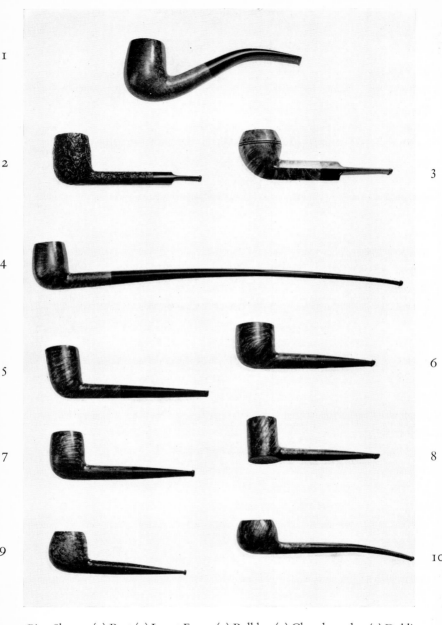

Pipe Shapes: (1) Bent (2) Lovat Frazer (3) Bulldog (4) Churchwarden (5) Dublin
(6) Pot (7) Billiard (8) Stand-up Poker (9) Apple (10) Prince

(*facing page 125*)

¶ *The Shape of the Pipe*

Vanity may have its influence on the shape of most things that a man chooses, but in the case of pipes it is more important to find one that is comfortable in the mouth than one which is pleasing to the eye; with a little care and trouble, however, both should be possible.

The ' Billiard ' is undoubtedly the most popular shape since it has pleasing and well-balanced proportions, and in the wall of the bowl and in the stem it carries plenty of wood. The term ' Billiard ', however, simply refers to its shape, and such pipes can be found in a number of sizes. The ' Apple ' and the ' Prince ' are examples of smaller, lighter bowls, and the slight curve in the stem of the 'Prince' helps to reduce the weight in the mouth. It should be noted that all curved stems have this effect, and many smokers find that a comparatively heavy 'bent' pipe is more comfortable than a long-stemmed ' straight ' pipe. Heavy bowls that lean forward tend to have the opposite effect; the leverage on the teeth is slightly increased. Some find that the shapes with cut-away or 'saddle' mouthpieces (such as the 'Bulldog' and 'Lovat Frazer') give a firmer grip and make it possible to use a heavier bowl than they would otherwise find comfortable.

It is important to remember that the bowl should carry not less than 1/16th of an inch of carbon. A bowl which appears to be a satisfactory size when new may later become so small that it is difficult to fill and, as a result of faulty packing, the tobacco does not burn evenly. A small pipe, though it is likely to have thin wood, may be satisfactory for a man who smokes a finely cut tobacco, but

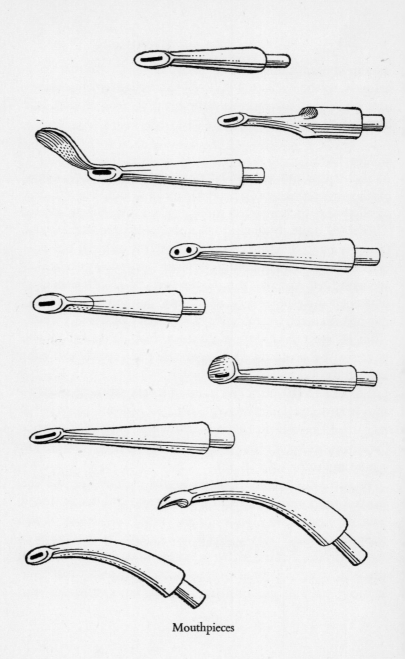

Mouthpieces

may be unsatisfactory for, say, a broadly cut 'Mixture' or a roughly rubbed 'Flake'. When selecting a bowl it is therefore important to remember the type of tobacco that will be smoked in it.

¶ *Mouthpieces*

Amber, imitation amber, horn, tortoiseshell, ivory, bone, plastic – there are many types of mouthpiece, but the best of all to-day are cut from blocks of compressed vulcanite. These are light, hygienic, tasteless, easily repairable, and they give a jet black glossy ' finish '. It should be remembered, however, that cheaper vulcanite mouthpieces which are moulded and less tough, are sometimes varnished so that their quality can be deceptive. Subject to this fact, mouthpieces can be judged by the quality of their ' finish '. Though even the cheapest are smoothed and polished, the lines from the mould may sometimes be seen on the sides and on the ' button '.

Comfort is the principal point. The mouthpiece must fit snugly and firmly between the teeth. A 'fish-tail' shape helps to spread the weight over several teeth, but, on the other hand, a mouthpiece that rocks because it is too wide makes a pipe unsatisfactory for smoking.

A narrow aperture will naturally concentrate all the smoke upon a limited area of the tongue and the pipe will seem to smoke very ' hot '. This in fact is a defect of the cheaper type of ' clay ' which lacks a special mouthpiece. At the other extreme, there are special shapes with holes at the side or the top which direct the smoke away from the sensitive parts of the tongue; and these are sometimes preferred by 'wet' smokers. Some people who have difficulty in finding a mouthpiece that will resist their bite select an extra thick 'lip'; in fact, it is better to use a thin, hand-cut mouthpiece that requires less pressure to keep it in place. If necessary, a silver 'lip' can be fitted.

There are various shapes designed with cut-away or turned-up 'lips' in order to give additional comfort to those with false-teeth. Smokers with this difficulty should be particularly careful to choose a pipe which they find to be well balanced.

¶ Grain

Since the age and toughness of briar root is indicated by its grain, a bowl which shows clear, natural markings is likely to have been cut from an old root that has had to struggle for existence; it should therefore contain the minimum of oil and sap. Thus it should be strong, heat resistant and likely to produce a cool smoke.

The pattern of grain that should be selected is, however, largely a matter of taste. The connoisseur, prepared to pay a large sum, may demand a 'straight grain' which, without irregularities and bare patches, runs parallel to the sides of the bowl over the whole surface. Such bowls have great aesthetic value and, being rare and expensive, become the choice pieces in any collection of modern pipes; but, in the opinion of many, they do not necessarily possess better smoking qualities or more strength than bowls with an irregular or mottled grain. Strength, a vital quality in every pipe, does not depend so much on the pattern of the grain as upon the quality of the wood, its thickness in both bowl and shank, the accuracy of the boring and the precision with which the mouthpiece is fitted. All this can often be found in a 'cross-grained' or mottled bowl, or in one which is well marked with 'birds-eye' – small, circular patches of light and dark grain.

The 'finish' of the bowl may be light or dark, but it is more important to determine its quality and, by examining the bowl in a strong light, to remain undeceived by varnishing processes which, in cheaper pipes, conceal flaws, very fine cracks and fillings that are liable to become apparent as the varnish wears off. Though the burning of sap and varnish can ruin the taste of the tobacco, the pipe's smoking qualities are not necessarily impaired by fillings. They simply indicate that the bowl has been cut from indifferent briar and, if the flaws are serious, its life may be short. Good quality pipes, it should be remembered, have a natural 'finish' that does not wear off.

A few bowls are not coloured at all. These darken pleasantly with smoking and there is no difficulty in giving them a close inspection when they are new. In the case of bowls with a rough or gnarled 'finish', it is important to distinguish between those which have been roughened by simpler methods and those which have been treated with expensive processes. In the latter, the natural grain remains after the softer wood has been removed by high pressure sand jets; the cheaper pipes, which are usually more rugged in appearance, have the whole of the bowl roughened in a more haphazard fashion by the teeth of a milling cutter. Apart from the pleasing appearance of all such pipes, lightness is their principal advantage.

In view of all this, the novice may rightly think that the successful choice of a pipe designed for his particular requirements presents a difficult task. There is of course no short cut to experience and, if he wishes to avoid unnecessary risks, he will do well to make his choice among the first class pipes of the many reputable manufacturers, for these, apart from being reliable, are often subject to a written guarantee.

(b) MAINTENANCE, CLEANLINESS AND CARE OF PIPES
¶ *Breaking-in the New Pipe*

A first-class, hard-grained pipe requires no breaking-in. If the wood has been properly seasoned, the bowl should give satisfactory results from the first filling. In the pipe of poor quality, however, there are saps and oil which have to be forced out by heat; the more there are, the more disagreeable is the task. In any case, a carbon deposit, which insulates the bowl from the heat of the burning tobacco, has to be formed and this should take place naturally in the course of smoking the pipe ten or twelve times. If carbon does not cling to the inside of the bowl readily, it is helpful to smear a little honey or molasses over it; this may also help to prevent unnecessary burning of the wood. Some Frenchmen use oil for this purpose, but by one Englishman, at any rate, the taste is not to be recommended.

To avoid over-heating, the bowl should be half filled for the first six smokes, packed and lit evenly and the pipe should be smoked indoors – not outside in a wind. The tobacco should be pressed down and smoked to the last shred so that the carbon covers the whole of the inside of the bowl. Before the bowl is emptied with a suitable instrument, it is better to allow a new pipe to cool, and it should certainly not be smoked again for several hours. Some smokers torture themselves unnecessarily by trying to 'break-in' an indifferent pipe in a single day.

¶ *Cleaning*

No one who values the pleasure of pipe-smoking will allow a pipe to become foul, but long before this unpleasant condition arises the purity and taste of the smoke deteriorates because the pores in the wood become saturated with 'tars'. Pipes in constant use and when smoking at their best require daily cleaning. While a pipe is warm (but not hot), it should be cleaned with a chenille pipe-cleaner, and some smokers prefer to leave this inside the stem throughout the night. In any case, the pipe should always be left in a tray or rack with the bowl downwards.

Periodically, say once a month, pipes should be cleaned thoroughly. This includes cutting the carbon with a reamer – and not with a penknife, which scrapes unevenly, damages and, in time, cuts through the base of the bowl. A wall of carbon 1/16" to 1/8" thick should be left (a big bowl can safely carry the larger amount), but the carbon should never be allowed to exceed 3/16". This is because the wood, after smoking, contracts more quickly than the carbon and a pipe that is resting with an excessive quantity of carbon in the bowl is liable to crack.

The mouthpiece, shank, base of the bowl and any metal tube or filter, if fitted, should be cleaned with a chenille cleaner or feather dipped in methylated spirit or, preferably, in any of the special preparations which are sold for the purpose. It is important not to allow these cleaning liquids to touch the outside of the pipe or the surface may be damaged. The stem and inside of the bowl should be dried with several fresh cleaners. (Neither water nor steam, which have an adverse effect on both the inside and outside of the pipe, should ever be used.)

Pipes that have been neglected or which have begun to smell musty after a long period of idleness can sometimes be revived by repeating the cleaning and drying several times. Such pipes should then be left for several days in the air so that the remining ' tars ' can evaporate.

The outside of the bowl and mouthpiece of a well-made pipe can be polished easily with a soft cloth. For older pipes a little wax polish may be helpful, and there are special preparations sold by tobacconists for this purpose.

During cleaning, the value of the simpler type of metal filter can be realised. Though some smokers prefer not to use them, they collect the juices and ' tars ' which other-wise cling to the bowl and stem and thus make cleaning a simpler task. All pipes can of course be cleaned and pro-cessed by a reputable tobacconist. A smoker who has not the time or inclination to look after his pipes is well advised to have them serviced regularly by an expert. The cost is small and the improvement to the pipe remarkable.

(c) THE CHOICE OF TOBACCO

Although the high prices of good quality tobaccos restrict the choice for many smokers, there is a wide variety of brands at any particular price, from the cheapest to the most expensive; and too many smokers are content to sample only a few which are sold at the price they wish to pay. Pipe-smoking has been said to be a sign of a phlegmatic, conservative temperament; whether or not this is true, habit certainly seems to dominate most smokers in their choice of tobacco. This is not surprising perhaps in the case of a man who has been smoking for many years and who, having sampled most brands at one time or another, has settled down to a steady, unwavering consumption of the best tobacco he can afford. But this certainly is not true of every pipe smoker. Many have never found a tobacco which gives total satisfaction or, having found it, do not necessarily want to smoke it all day long. A ' Mixture ' which gives great pleasure after dinnner may seem a little rich or exotic during the rigours of morning work. An Empire ' Flake ' or ' Navy Cut ' which serves as an adequate tobacco during the day may, conversely, seem a little flat and dull in the evening. Variety and contrast can obviously add to the pleasures of pipe smoking. Moreover, many expensive tobaccos are economical in the sense that they contain a relatively lower moisture content and therefore last longer. Any reputable tobacconist can give advice on these questions and, in many cases, provide tobaccos which are designed to meet individual requirements.

From the many standard brands of ' Flakes ', ' Navy Cuts ' and ' Spun Cuts ' to the various types of ' Mixture ', there are many possibilities open to the adventurous smoker, and the reader who wishes to be reminded of the principal brands may refer to Chapter III. No arbitrary advice can usefully be given on the question of strength and aroma; by taste, trial and error, every smoker must decide for himself. One common mistake may, however, be pointed out. Novices or ardent cigarette smokers who wish to experiment with a pipe often make the assumption that they should begin with a *mild* tobacco. This can lead to disaster, for a mild tobacco, especially if it is finely cut and smoked rapidly – the inevitable mistake of those unaccustomed to a pipe – can taste very hot and burn the tongue. It is safer to begin with a 'Navy Cut' or 'Mixture' of medium strength which is not cut too fine and which is neither too moist nor too dry.

The man who smokes quickly and nervously, or one who is constantly smoking out of doors so that his pipe is exposed to the wind, is likely to get more satisfaction from a coarsely cut, slow burning tobacco of medium strength. For the sportsman who is continually in the open air some form of windshield for the bowl is a distinct advantage because this, by minimising the draught on the bowl, keeps the pipe cooler and makes the tobacco burn more slowly. At the other extreme, a man who prefers to draw at his pipe very slowly will find that a finely cut tobacco has the merit of burning evenly and steadily with the minimum of effort on his part.

The way in which a particular tobacco will burn depends on its quality, its cut, the amount of moisture it contains and how it is packed in the bowl. Tobacco which is bought in paper packets and kept in a pouch in a warm pocket cannot be expected to keep its condition. Unless a smoker prefers his tobacco to be dry – and this is sometimes the case, especially with smokers of 'Mixtures' – it should be bought in airtight tins and kept in an airtight jar. But tobacco which has lost its original condition has not always been spoilt irreparably. A piece of blotting-paper, moistened with water and left in the tobacco tin for 24 hours, can restore dry tobacco successfully. Even a slice of potato in the pouch is a well known safeguard. Some smokers like to spray their tobacco with rum, various essences and even with water. But there is always the danger of increasing the moisture content so much that the tobacco fails to burn properly.

¶ Pipe Smoking in General

In past centuries pipe-smoking was enjoyed at leisure. It was a practice that merited and received a little ceremony and a good deal of care. Though the tempo of modern life has had its effect even upon the handling of pipes, the man who has no time or interest for the finer points is undoubtedly squandering his pleasure. Anyone can smoke; it is a simple enough action. But comparatively few know how to obtain the utmost pleasure from their smoking. To the experienced, the whole matter may be instinctive – below the level of thought; but the inexperienced may do well to attend to a few simple points which follow.

¶ Filling

It is important to fill the bowl slowly and evenly, *lightly* pressing down each pinch of tobacco. If the particular brand can be fed into the bowl in a continuous stream, this helps it to burn evenly. Every tobacco, moreover, requires a slightly different touch so that, when filled, the pipe has a firm steady draw that imposes no strain on the lips. It is important to test the draw and to repack the bowl if necessary, for most of the unsatisfactory smoking that requires the pipe to be lit again and again is due to careless filling. The surface tobacco should not be pressed down, but left slightly loose or even teased out with the fingers so that it will accept the flame readily. ('Spun-Cut' needs particularly careful packing.) Some smokers, especially if they tend to collect moisture in the pipe, make use of a small metal plug which fits neatly into the bottom of the bowl so that a small gap under the tobacco improves the draw. Others find that the packing of the tobacco in specially prepared pipe-papers facilitates slow, even burning. If, however, the pipe has been packed too tightly, the draw can sometimes be improved by clearing an air space with a pen-knife or pipe-tool; but it is usually more satisfactory to scoop out the tobacco and refill.

¶ *Lighting*

It is important to light the whole surface of the tobacco with a strong, broad flame. Most cigarette lighters have too weak a flame to light a heavy tobacco and, as a result, the pipe does not draw properly and has to be lit again and again. After lighting, the tobacco should be pressed down to the level of the top of the bowl. While smoking the use of a suitable stopper is important, for unless the ash is shaken off periodically and the remaining tobacco pressed down, continual relighting will be necessary. (A finger placed over the bowl is a simple method of increasing the draught).

When relighting, the charred tobacco and ash should be loosened with the spoon of a pipe-tool, tapped out gently and the remaining tobacco pressed down. When applying the light, a slight blow through the stem (in addition to the customary draw) will prevent rank fumes from entering the mouth, and will help the tobacco to light more easily if it has become moist.

¶ *After Smoking*

The moist 'dottle' and remaining strands of tobacco which can quickly make the pipe foul should be removed with the spoon of a pipe-tool. The bowl may be tapped lightly against the palm of the hand, if necessary, but it is a pathetic misuse of any pipe to tap it against hard objects which chip the bowl and run serious risk of snapping the peg in the stem. A pipe was never designed as a hammer and will give poor service as such. Though it is important to empty the bowl at once, the mouthpiece of a warm pipe should not be removed immediately because the stem contracts slightly with heat and may split if the mouthpiece is twisted out forcibly.

If they are to give of their best, pipes require constant rest. They should not be refilled and smoked again until cold, and whenever possible, should be put into a rack, bowl downwards, so that the carbon will absorb any moisture and the air can thoroughly dry the bowl. It is harmful to the pipe – if not unhygienic – to keep it in the pocket indefinitely or shut up in a closed drawer or box for long periods. The pipe that is not allowed to rest in the fresh air will gradually begin to taste bitter and its qualities will slowly deteriorate. For these reasons the most satisfactory results are achieved by smoking a number of pipes in rotation.

CIGARS

¶ *On Offering and Choosing a Cigar*

Boxes should be opened carefully with the special blunt-bladed tool that cannot damage the cigars. Penknives are dangerous for this purpose. Cigars in bundles should be lifted from and returned to their boxes by means of the ribbon or, when packed flat in rows, they should be taken out individually by pressing lightly on the rounded head, thus raising the opposite end. The amateur who attempts to lift them straight from the box with finger and thumb is likely to damage the 'wrapper'.

The only sure test for a cigar is to smoke it, but experience makes it possible to conjecture what it is one is about to smoke. Although the 'wrapper' should be smooth, firm, without prominent veins and neatly finished at the head, it is only one part of the cigar. Its paleness does not necessarily mean that the 'filler' is mild also, although, as a general rule, darker leaf always tends to be stronger. A few light spots (sometimes caused on the growing 'wrapper' leaf by dew which has been dried in the sun) are of no consequence, and there is little to be learnt from the popular practice of sniffing at the cigar, or of placing it close to the ear where a faint crackle can be heard even in a cigar that is immature. The novice who wants to enjoy a cigar should select one that is not too big – a Half Corona size is suggested – and, after examining the 'wrapper', the only other test is to press it gently with the fingers. It should feel even and firm throughout its whole length; if it feels soft, it is probably immature or badly filled; a brittle crackling is an obvious sign of dryness. After experience it is possible to discover whether the 'filler' is uniform.

¶ *On Preparing and Smoking a Cigar*

Since every smoker of experience has his own fads and foibles, in the matter of smoking it is dangerous to be dogmatic. So much is a matter of taste and opinion. Nevertheless, there are a few important points which give the cigar a chance to offer its best.

After pressing the band lightly with the fingers and thumb all the way round, it should be torn off carefully so that the 'wrapper' is not damaged.

Although there are various ways of piercing the butt end, some of them may damage the 'wrapper' and produce an unsatisfactory aperture. Much depends on the condition of the cigar. In the United States it is customary to bite off the end of ' green ' (or fresh) cigars. When handling mature cigars, some smokers crack open the end by squeezing it between finger and thumb, but unless the cigar is in excellent condition and the butt perfectly made, this can be disastrous. Many prefer to use a cigar piercer and take care to tap out any broken fragments of leaf; although, by exposing the minimum amount of ' filler ', this method helps the ' wrapper ' to keep tobacco tar away from the tongue, the smoke and moisture concentrate in one narrow passage and may result in a bad draw.

Perhaps the most satisfactory method is a clean ' V ' shaped cut made by a cigar-cutter, because this ensures the removal of broken leaf and provides a passage for the smoke that does not concentrate all of it upon a small area of the tongue. It is unwise to blow through a cigar in order to remove particles of broken leaf because this injects moisture from the breath. – The tip of a pointed shape should be removed with a straight cutter or turned against the blade of a sharp knife and cut straight across. Some experts like to prepare cigars of every shape in the same way.

The broad flame of a match or spill is the most satisfactory for lighting, and this should be done carefully and without hurry. Some smokers prefer to hold the tip in the flame until it glows evenly and then gently to draw in enough smoke to fill only the cigar. If this is expelled through the cigar, no smoke made harsh by lighting can spoil the palate. Whatever method of preparation may be preferred, there is no doubt that careful lighting and slow smoking are the only ways to ensure that the cigar burns evenly; if it does not, the only remedy is to smoke as slowly as possible until the shape of the ash becomes uniform. The retention of the ash helps to keep the smoke cool, but, although it should not flake, the length of the ash will depend on the cutting of the ' filler ' and not necessarily on its quality. White ash does not denote the best cigars, for Havanas produce an ash that is steel-grey in colour.

A cigar in good condition should not go out during smoking. If, however, relighting is necessary, it is advisable to rub off the charred end with a match until it is level and then, as the flame is applied, to draw very gently in the way that has already been suggested. This will ensure that rank fumes contaminate the palate and the rest of the cigar as little as possible.

¶ *The Care and Keeping of Cigars*

Choice and expensive cigars, which are made with such skill and labour, require far more attention than they often receive. On account of the sensitive and absorbent quality of the leaf they should be bought and stored in small quantities and in a constant temperature of 60° – 65° F; they need protection just as much from draughts and smells as from the quick drying effects of central heating. They can even become contaminated by the smell of soap from the hands. Since too much heat spoils their quality and damp produces mould, humidors, designed to keep them in perfect condition, are always a wise investment. In a room where a number of boxes are to be stored, a cedar-wood cabinet is essential for this wood affords the best protection and yet allows the process of maturing to continue. Thus the lids of boxes should be firmly closed after each cigar has been removed. 'Green' cigars (or 'fresh', as Americans sometimes call them) should be kept in aluminium tubes, cellophane wrappings or glass jars in order to preserve their freshness.

As long as cigars carry a faint sheen on the surface of the 'wrapper' they are probably in good condition, but if they are soft to the touch, they are still probably 'green' and, except for those who prefer them in this state, they need to be kept in the correct conditions for several months. From the time they are packed in the 'green' state, cigars may take up to a year to reach full maturity. Through the slight sweating that they undergo during this period the contents of some boxes may be found to be covered with a fine grey powdery deposit called 'bloom'; this is not harmful if it is removed with a soft camel-hair brush. Those which have been allowed to become dry should never be moistened, and cigars which, through excessive damp, have begun to smell musty have been spoilt irreparably and should be thrown away. There is no remedy for a failure of this kind. To give the care and attention which avoids such disasters is to understand the delicate nature of cigars and the immense pleasure they offer to those who treat them well.

SHORT BIBLIOGRAPHY

APPERSON, G. L., The Social History of Smoking (London 1914)

ARENTS, G, Jr., Tobacco (5 vols: New York 1937)

BRYANT & MAY, Museum of Fire-Making Appliances (London 1926)

CORTI, Count, A History of Smoking (London 1931)

CURTIS, Prof. M. M., The History of Snuff and Snuff Boxes, (New York 1935)

DUNHILL, Alfred, The Pipe Book (London 1924)

FAIRHOLT, F. W., Tobacco, Its History and Associations, 1859

GARNER, W. W. G., The Production of Tobacco (New York 1951)

McCAUSLAND, H., Snuff and Snuff-Boxes (London 1951)

PENN, W. A., The Soverane Herb (London 1901)

INDEX